PEGUY

PEGUY

by

ALEXANDER DRU

LONDON

THE HARVILL PRESS

Published by
THE HARVILL PRESS LTD.
23 Lower Belgrave Street
London, S.W.1

1956

Printed in Great Britain
by W. & J. Mackay & Co. Ltd, Chatham

CONTENTS

(deepening, fathoming)

I

THE APPROACH TO PEGUY

*Tu ne me lirais pas si
tu ne m'avais déjà compris.*

VALERY: *Lettre sur Mallarmé.*

Charles Péguy is a name in English-speaking countries and little more. He is not unknown, but his fame is curiously in the air, unanchored to any very precise achievement. His reputation in France is therefore something of an enigma, and it is usually assumed that his personality contributed as much to his fame as his ideas, his prose and his poetry. Not much has been written about him in English, and he is almost always discussed as though his poetry were a secondary consideration, one sphere of activity among others in which he made an impression.

Péguy, it is true, only began writing poetry towards the end of his life, six years before his death, and this imposes an unusual chronological division on his work which has probably contributed to creating the impression that there are other equally important factors in his life to be taken into account: his political and social ideas, his pamphlets and polemics, and his religious conversion. And once that point of view has taken root, it is only a step to regarding his poetry as a by-product of his genius.

In the following pages I have reversed the order. If Péguy was a poet and not just a writer who also wrote poetry, his work as a whole will only be accessible through his poetry. It is not the poet's thought which explains his poetry, as though he had merely put his ideas into verse; his poetry qualifies his thought decisively. *Tu ne me lirais pas si tu ne m'avais déjà compris* is eminently true of Péguy, and one of the functions of his poetry is to establish the current of sympathy which deepens understanding beyond the level of discursive argument. Without that 'Open Sesame' the reader may look in vain for the key. With it he enters into the poet's world.

Péguy's fame rests on his power to communicate his vision. It may not be impossible to approach him in some other way, and some wholly irrelevant factor may suddenly reveal the unity of his work. But in point of fact Péguy's thought has not made much headway outside his own country, largely, I think, because he is not regarded first and foremost as a poet. In any other light Péguy seems more eccentric than original, more negative than positive, not infrequently because his ideas are lifted from the form in which they live, and fitted into some existing scheme of thought which deprives them of vitality.

The general opinion of Péguy seems indeed to be that he was an eccentric, one of a fairly numerous family, who reacted against the contemporary world, and shut themselves up in an angry Catholicism, bristling with distaste for the existing order. A familiar, amusing and interesting class.

Only Péguy is anything but amusing, and 'interesting' is precisely what he is not. There was nothing of the aesthete or the intellectual about him. *Un bon français de l'espèce ordinaire*, his life falls flat in the telling of it, and he makes a poor show in the class in which he is usually judged. That is one of the reasons why he is not read much in England or, I think, America.

Péguy certainly is an eccentric, perhaps *the* eccentric of French literature. But, paradoxically enough, through remaining at the centre of tradition. This accounts for his being treated both as a traditionalist and as a revolutionary, a reactionary and a progressive, or even as an amalgam of the two. His point of view was an enigma to most of those who knew him, and it is not surprising that approached from the angle of his political, social and religious ideas, which are entangled in the conflict that befuddled his generation during the Dreyfus Affair, he should be found not only difficult, but dull. Many of his contemporaries felt the same.

Success was slow in coming to him, and when it came it was intangible; a *succès d'estime* that left him as isolated as before and his wife with the butcher's bill. But when he was killed at the head of his company, in the first days of the Battle of the Marne, the force behind the enigma was widely acknowledged. *Périr inachevé dans un combat militaire*, he had written. The death for which he had prepared as an officer of the reserve, and as a poet, seemed to set a seal on his life and work and gave it form and significance.

Immediately after the war Péguy's *Oeuvres Complètes* were issued in a fine edition which would have pleased the poet who attached as much importance to the type-face and the lay-out as Mallarmé himself. The introductions are less satisfactory. Millerand, Barrès and Suarès speak with one voice, but at the critical point they are so vague that their praise sounds like an official tribute. Péguy, they exclaim, is a hero, a saint, a prophet. Nevertheless Péguy's reputation was slow to spread. As late as 1931 Emmanuel Mounier was still writing in the future when he said that so great a poet, so profound a thinker, so prophetic a mind 'would one day be recognised at his true value'. The second war again focused attention on Péguy's work and he came into his own. There was no longer any doubt about his importance, but when Romain Rolland wrote his

Péguy he could not avoid calling him a prophet, and
Bernanos did his best not to call him a saint. 'I do not regard him as a saint exactly, but as a man who, although
dead, remains within our reach, or even nearer, at our beck
and call, who answers when one speaks to him.' His true
value was on the way to becoming clear.

Such uninhibited phrases only serve to put the English
reader on his guard. The French convention is different.
The praise that has been heaped on Péguy is unqualified
because of the difficulty of analysing his true value. His
faults are after all obvious. What is not so easy to determine
is his 'true value'. To call him a hero, a saint or a prophet
was the shortest way of saying that he was all of a piece.
He was not a *maître*, with a doctrine, nor an influence in
the literary world, but an unpredictable force whose value
lay as much in the future as in his work.

It is neither as hero, nor as saint, nor as prophet that
Péguy is likely to cross the Channel and be understood.
Péguy is a poet, and it is as a poet that he becomes accessible, because it is the poet who is the author of the whole
work, both prose and verse. It is not the thought or the
form of Péguy's work that is difficult, but its unity, which
means to say that it must be seen as a whole. His thought,
his politics, his social ideas are co-ordinated by the poet in
him and more precisely by his conception of imagination
and of communication. Even his religious faith is characterised by the form in which it is communicated. The
key to Péguy is, to repeat, his poetry, and it alone supplies
the point of view for everything he said, wrote and did.

And because Péguy only began to write poetry late in
life, it is possible to follow the gradual clarification of his
conception of poetry, and it is the genesis of his poetic
work which opens the door to his world. His life, his

battles, his friendships and quarrels, his conversion itself are liable to become so many false scents if they are used as guides to Péguy's mind. His poetry, on the other hand, is the vanishing point in the picture on which proportion and perspective rest. From that point it is possible to see Péguy as whole and all of a piece. Poets are born, not made, and as the first *Jeanne d'Arc* shows, Péguy was a poet from the first whose poetry, by a freak of nature, only came to fruition late in his life. This makes it possible to follow the growth of the poet's mind until it matured in his poetry, and with the help of that co-ordinating thread to see his work as he saw it. To approach him *via* his politics, his philosophy, his Catholicism even, is inevitably to impose a different background on his thought. Coleridge after all wrote voluminously on religion, politics and philosophy, but his work as a whole can only be seen through his conception of poetry.

A study of the poet, of his notion of poetry and of certain aspects of his poetic works is not, I should add, a biography. Whether the two could be profitably combined in Péguy's case is an open point. Of the biographies and studies which have so far appeared, and which attempt to penetrate his thought from the standpoint of psychology, none seems to me to have produced valuable results. Romain Rolland's two volumes, by far the most finished portrait which has yet appeared, avoid making that mistake, if it is one. Rolland's success is due to the fact that his study is instinctively ordered and coloured by his feeling for the writer, his limitations to an inadequate understanding of Péguy's poetry.*

*Romain Rolland is an invaluable guide to Péguy's work which he follows in chronological order from beginning to end. While remaining on the surface he handles the enormous mass of detail with consummate

The relation between tradition and freedom is one of the central themes of Péguy's work. It appears in the earliest *Cahiers*, and long before he saw it consciously as a poet. It happened, however, to be the problem uppermost in the minds of his contemporaries who saw it from an exclusively political angle. Péguy was thus plunged into the violent debates of the Dreyfus Affair and began using words in a new sense and, moreover, in a sense which was to lead him in a direction which at first he did not understand. His thought, in fact, was coloured by his conception of poetry long before that conception became clear to him. And it was this hidden misunderstanding, more than any differences of opinion, which involved him in a series of acrimonious debates in which his opponents sometimes seemed to him to pervert his meaning wilfully. It is not his quick temper which explains his quarrels, but his difficulties of language which made them inevitable. The more explicit he became the more eccentric and paradoxical he seemed. He refused to be lumped with the traditionalists or the progressives. He wanted the best of both worlds and in his poetry tried to express it.

---

skill and his personal knowledge of the period enriches the biographical portrait and brings it to life.

The first and, I think, the only complete study in depth of Péguy's work is *Le Prophète Péguy* (1946). In a series of studies, *Le poète de la vie, Le poète de la naissance, Le poète de l'honneur,* Rousseaux abandons the chronological order and concentrates on the structure of Péguy's world excluding all biographical and historical material. In a sense the two works are complementary.

A third method of approaching Péguy is revealed in *L'Eve de Péguy* by Albert Béguin whose close analysis of Péguy's epic *Eve* performs roughly the same task as Rousseaux's more general work.

All three writers have contributed to a better understanding of Péguy, in particular the last two named, and I should like to acknowledge my debt to all three which the form of this essay precludes my doing in detail.

II

EARLY YEARS

Before turning to Péguy's work, the story of his early years may be briefly recalled. He was born in Orleans on 7th January, 1873. His father, a carpenter by trade, employing one or two men, died shortly after his son's birth, and Péguy was brought up by his mother who supplemented her slender means by re-caning chairs. Péguy's grandmother, who lived with them, he liked to think, could neither read nor write with any ease. He was sent to school in Orleans, and a discerning master (whom Péguy afterwards thanked in the *Cahiers*) saw that he tried for a scholarship to the secondary school. Not without difficulty he passed his examinations and in 1891 was sent to the Lycée Lakanal at Sceaux. It was while he was at the Lycée that he gave up the practice of his religion.

At his first attempt to get into the university, he failed and decided to volunteer for military service. At the end of his year in the army he passed into the Sorbonne, entering in 1894, after a period at the Collège Sainte-Barbe where we first see him in the Tharauds' pages, obstinate, intense and burning with idealism. By the time he went to the Sorbonne he had already begun to interest himself in the socialist movement and was active in good works. As the Dreyfus Affair got under way he threw himself into it and was the first to dash from his study and join in a rough-house with the 'Talas',* the anti-Dreyfusards. But within a

---

*'Talas', those who went to Mass—'qui vont-à-la Messe'. There was a substantial neo-Catholic movement at this date.

year Péguy applied for a long vacation on the transparently false grounds that his sight was deteriorating, although he was warned that the interruption might well cost him his degree, as in fact it did. He went back to Orleans with the famous black-japanned box that had mystified his roommates for some time back. On his return he produced the almost completed manuscript of the first *Jeanne d'Arc*, an enormous historical pageant, the point of which entirely escaped his friends, who thought him taken up with Dreyfus and Socialism.

That initial misunderstanding marks the beginning of his career, and of his isolation. Not that he ever lacked friends. But even his intimates were never allowed into his secret. The sheer idealism and assertiveness of the *Cahiers* tends to conceal *notre cher Péguy*, the infectious enthusiasm and courage that drew a very varied group of friends into his wake. They might not ever know quite clearly where he was going or even precisely where he was, but the authority with which he led them never deprived them or him of freedom.

Péguy's first prose work, *Marcel: premier dialogue de la cité harmonieuse*, was inspired by his school friend Marcel Baudouin. Baudouin had died at the end of 1896. How much Péguy owed him can never be known, but their relationship can be guessed from all Péguy's friendships, with Herr, Sorel, Halévy, Maritain, Benda and others. His works, as Suarès says, are a perpetual dialogue between Péguy and his friends. He listened and learnt, and they often thought they were the paramount influence in his life, till he suddenly appeared in a new guise, the one they had least expected. In the end it was he who led the way, even when they did not follow.

In the year following Marcel Baudouin's death, Péguy

married Baudouin's sister. With his wife's agreement, they sank her *dot* in a small publishing business, the Librairie Georges Bellais. *Jeanne d'Arc* was published, and one or two copies were sold. The remainder were heaped up round the shop and served as benches. Péguy had his head-quarters. He had set off at a good pace, like his Descartes, *ce cavalier français qui partit d'un si bon pas*. He was always a man of decision. He had left college to do his military service; he left the university to write *Jeanne d'Arc*; he threw himself into the Dreyfus Affair; he married and sank everything in a publishing venture which was hopeless from the start. His liberty was always to be the fruit of action and of irrevocable decisions, of his courage and *fidélité*, the courage to break with the past and fidelity to the past.

Péguy's courage and fidelity were tested in the Dreyfus Affair which opened in 1894 and dragged on in one form or another for ten years, covering the whole period of his youth down to his return to Catholicism. He seems at times to invest it with a disproportionate importance, and then in the end he would dismiss it and everything he had written about it as of no importance. At one moment he seems to take a wholly subjective view of the incident, and it is not until the Dreyfus Affair is seen, as he saw it, as the culmination of a whole period in French history, that his attitude becomes comprehensible and his course visible. The Dreyfus revolution was to him the end of the old order and the beginning of the new; it forced him to break with the immediate past and re-discover the historical unity of France.

In the posthumously published version of *Clio* (the second version on which he was working at the date of his death) Péguy sums up his conclusions:

D'une âme paienne on peut faire une âme chrétienne ... De l'âme de la veille on peut faire l'âme du jour. Mais celui qui n'a pas de veille, comment lui ferait-on un lendemain ... C'est du monde paien que fut fait le monde chrétien, et nullement d'un zéro de monde. C'est de la cité paienne que fut faite la cité chrétienne, et non pas, et nullement, d'un zéro de cité.

He was not alone in discovering the *zéro de cité*, the lack of soul, the failure of the modern city in the Dreyfus Affair. The Dreyfus Affair itself was proof of the weakness of the Republic. It assumed its fantastic proportions because all those involved—and everyone was involved—had consciously or unconsciously recognised the weakness and corruption of the Republic. But with hardly an exception they tried to bolster up their positions by returning to the ideas and ideologies which had created the situation. Péguy was one of the few who had the courage to break with the past, with the Socialists and the Catholics, the Left and the Right, without losing sight of the deeper lessons which the Affair taught him. The Dreyfus Affair is the arena in which Péguy clarified the issues before his generation and there is no escape but to consider as briefly as possible the nexus of historical ideas which it presented to him as it unrolled.

III

THE DREYFUS AFFAIR

The Dreyfus Affair was the grand finale to a hundred years' war. 'From the eighteenth century to the present day,' Professor Butterfield writes, 'Roman Catholicism on the one hand, and the more liberal or progressive parties on the other, have split the French tradition from top to bottom, producing a cleavage which has extended over much of the continent.' That cleavage found its final expression in the Dreyfus Affair. The split in the French tradition had been completed in the eighteenth century, but it was crystallised politically, and sanctified by the Revolution, and further confirmed by the reaction which followed during the Restoration. It was then that 'the religious question' became the hub around which all other questions revolved. The failure to clarify and distinguish the several issues involved led to an over-simplification of the problem which virtually allowed of no solution except unending and embittered strife.

The Revolution had despoiled the Church of its enormous wealth and great privileges. Under Napoleon it had been reassembled and given the status and powers which he regarded as useful. With the return of the elder branch of the Bourbons the traditional alliance between the Throne and the Altar came into play as part of the return to 'normal conditions'. The underlying assumption that France was still a Catholic country, and that Catholicism could function from the steps of the Throne as it had always done, was not seriously examined by those in power and any opposition to the solution was attributed to revolutionary tendencies.

The first internal criticism of the alliance between Catholicism and Conservatism came from Lamennais, and his attitude did much to define how the question was viewed throughout the century. Félicité de Lamennais entered the Church late in life and left it comparatively early. His career lasted nearly twenty years; his fall was meteoric, against darkening skies. Lamennais's originality consisted in reversing the traditional policy. He followed de Maistre in advocating the closest of bonds between the Pope and the Church in France, thus breaking with the already defunct Gallican tradition; and outdistanced de Maistre by seeing that this implied a Church based on the people instead of on the Monarchy. For he saw that the Monarchy could not last. He sympathised with the liberal hopes and the democratic feelings of the people and looked forward to a progressive Papacy strengthened by its alliance with 'democracy'.

Lamennais's aim was the regeneration of society which he believed could only be brought about through a strong and united Catholicism. He wished to see Catholicism linked with the Left rather than with the Right, and his proposals amounted to a reversal of a millenary policy. He saw the social and political questions of the day quickly and clearly, and his desire to dissociate the Church from the failing Monarchy is so self-evidently reasonable that the alternative he proposed appears in rather too favourable and simple a light. As a thinker he belongs in the third rank of romantic philosophers, and no one has ever tried to raise him to the rank of theologian. He was not a revolutionary and perhaps not revolutionary enough. His religion and his politics were never sufficiently clearly articulated.

But he stands at the beginning of the period and helped to dictate the form in which 'the religious question' was seen from that time on. He aroused great enthusiasm; he failed to achieve his end, and left his Catholic opponents confirmed in the view that the alternative to a Catholicism of the Right was a Catholicism of the Left. He was politically minded himself, and his legacy was to ensure that the Catholics in France remained imprisoned in a political attitude and failed to go back to their sources for rejuvenation. More particularly, the conception of tradition was given a political character. The absence of serious philosophical or theological work, and the poverty of Catholic writing as a whole, during the ensuing period, are an illustration of the extent to which politics ousted all other interests and considerations.

The split in the French tradition was given permanence by the most effective method, gross over-simplification. After 1832, when Lamennais was condemned, the cleavage was represented as between Clerical and anti-Clerical parties. Liberal Catholicism ceased to play any rôle after 1848, and the work of liberal-minded men such as de Mun and Ozanam was carried out without seriously affecting the political issues. Neither Lacordaire nor Montalembert had any illusions about the failure of their hopes.

The degree to which the country was divided into Clerical and anti-Clerical parties is not easy to realise, and yet it played a capital part throughout the century and came to a head once again in the Dreyfus Affair. But unless the strength of prejudice is grasped, Péguy's reading of the Dreyfus Affair, his deliberate treatment of both sides as more or less identical, is bound to seem eccentric. Michelet, for example, the great representative of the revolutionary tradition, the author of *Le Peuple*, speaks of France as

divided into Two Nations, though not in Disraeli's sense
of the rich and the poor. Largely through Michelet's influence, the perpendicular, ideological division assumed a
reality and an importance which obscured the horizontal
cleavage, the fundamental social division. Under the Third
Republic 'the religious question' became the ruling factor
in politics.*

With the formation of a Clerical party under the Restoration the political scene was set and the Liberal opposition
knew that they were on to a good thing. Benjamin Constant was among the first to see how invaluable Clericalism
was to be to the Liberals and Progressives and what an in-
destructible bogy it provided. *Quand on n'a rien*, he said,
*eh bien! il reste les Jésuites. Je les sonne comme un valet de
chambre: ils arrivent toujours*. For the rest of the century the
clericals always provided the opposition with a target. As
long as the red-rag of Clericalism could be waved in the
Chamber and at the hustings, the red flag of Socialism
could be relegated to the background. Those who gained
from playing the political game were the wealthy and en-
lightened bourgeoisie who, using Constant's tactics, man-
aged to a remarkable degree to avoid the social problems
created by the industrialisation of France, and to impose a
socially conservative programme on the country by treating the perpendicular cleavage between rival ideologies as
the one important factor. The Catholics, moreover, played
into their hands and acquiesced in viewing the religious

*The extent of Michelet's influence may be gauged by the fact that
his lectures, published in conjunction with Quinet's, in 1843, created
such a heated atmosphere that Sainte-Beuve mentions their appearance
as one of the reasons for delaying the publication of the third volume of
Port-Royal. 'La question religieuse, comme on disait, prit feu de toutes
parts' and Sainte-Beuve despaired of obtaining a calm hearing for the
volume which dealt with the *Provinciales*.

questions from a political angle. The struggle which ensued centred round education, and in order to maintain a hold on the schools and the universities, the Catholics gave their support to any government which left them the powers and authority they claimed. Louis Napoleon saw the advantages which were to be drawn from this attitude and accorded them certain privileges in education. The Catholics found themselves committed to a régime which antagonised moderate liberal opinion in the country, and were associated with a foreign policy which ended in the disaster of Sedan.

The Third Republic, which was born in the following years, was a compromise between Right and Left based upon the fact that the essential dividing line was between Clericalism and anti-Clericalism. Thiers, who presided at its birth, had already shown that he could use clericalism with the same skill as Constant. Whenever the Revolution seemed to be gaining the upper hand, he gave the Clericals more rope, confident that they would both hold the revolution in check and subsequently hang themselves. He had opposed the Catholic demands in education in 1845. After the Revolution of 1848 he supported Falloux, and it was largely through his efforts that the education laws of 1850 were passed. But in 1873 he felt that the Commune had sufficiently frightened the radicals, and that there was no fear for the moment of further revolution. His unspoken agreement with Gambetta made it possible for him to prevent the return of the Monarchy without giving any ground to the rising demands of the small Socialist groups. Gambetta did his work for him by proclaiming that 'There is no social question' and adding that 'The social peril is Clericalism'. And since those sentiments were generally accepted, Thiers was able to baptise the Republic Conservative, while leaving it full scope to let off steam on the religious question.

But as social questions became more pressing, and the danger of Clericalism more remote, the equilibrium upon which the functioning of Thiers's Republic depended, was threatened. In Péguy's view all genuine belief in the Republic had died during the decade which preceded the Dreyfus Affair, and the violence of feeling which it generated was simply a sign of want of faith. No one believed in the Republic and the consequence was fanatical support to one of the two parties into which it had split.

When the Dreyfus Affair broke in the autumn of 1894, the Government of moderate Republicans was led by an uninspired politician, Jules Méline, who had made a competent Minister of Agriculture. On all sides there was a pious hope that the scandals and affairs of the last ten years might be forgotten. No party and hardly a single individual had escaped being implicated in one or more of the scabrous episodes.

The danger signal had been given when Boulanger, the most farcical political adventurer in modern times, had been swept on a wave of popularity to the verge of dictatorship. The ground of Boulanger's popularity was the widespread conviction that the Republic was hopelessly corrupt, and that only a strong man, almost regardless of his views, could pull France together again. Since Ferry's defeat at the hands of the radicals, Gambetta had exercised a sort of underground authority that held the Republicans together. But with Gambetta's early death in 1882 the field was left open to the charlatan. Boulanger's success was due solely to his ephemeral popularity and the use which the parties thought they could make of him. He was without ability, without talent and without scruple.

The creature of Clémenceau, who launched Boulboul as he called him, ended up as a dummy supported by the Right. But his inadequacy which no one denied, and his dishonesty which everyone knew, were overshadowed by a series of scandals.

The first large-scale scandal struck at the President of the Republic, when Jules Grévy's son-in-law, Daniel Wilson, was found to have been selling honours, using the Elysée Palace as his office. In the following year the Panama scandal broke and involved all parties. Its ramifications have never been cleared up, for even French public opinion discovered that there was a limit to the amount of dirty linen which it was politic to wash in public. But Clémenceau, for example, did not live down the suspicion of having been involved for ten years. The Right was in no better position, and having backed Boulanger's popular black horse, on which the Duchesse d'Uzès put three million, was left high and dry when Boulanger fled to Belgium and shot himself on his mistress's grave.

From 1881, which Péguy dates as the beginning of the *monde moderne*, the world without faith or soul, the situation in France had worsened. But in 1890 a certain *détente* was noticeable. It looked for a moment as though the religious question might be solved or at least shelved, when Leo XIII inaugurated his policy of *ralliement*; and *Immortale Dei* (1885) had been welcomed as a good omen. The Vatican policy was to end the struggle between the Catholics and the Republic, and was officially launched in 1891, but promptly torpedoed by the Catholics, for whom any such agreement was anathema. Nevertheless Méline still hoped that some *modus vivendi* might be discovered, and perhaps if Dreyfus had not been court-martialled and condemned, Leo's policy would have prevailed. Méline simply closed his eyes to the situation and refused to admit the importance of the Dreyfus Affair: *Il n'y a pas d'affaire Dreyfus*, he repeated, until it threw him out of office.

In fact there were three: the trial and re-trial of Alfred Dreyfus, accused of revealing military secrets to the German embassy; the political battle which developed round the trials; and the deeper changes which ultimately followed: the *révolution dreyfusienne*. For as a result of the Affair, the conservative Republic which Thiers had fathered on the country began to alter in character. The Socialists emerged as a party, and the social questions which had been kept in the background came to the fore with the spread of Marxist ideas and the formation of the powerful trade unions. The 'religious question' which had long ago ceased to correspond to the facts, gradually ceased to occupy the centre of the stage.

The Dreyfus Affair was the last time the old politico-religious forces dominated the scene, and the religious question in the form in which it had bedevilled French life since the revolution was effectively used. France, as Péguy said, was plunged into Wars of Religion, fought by men who believed in nothing. All the old prejudices were revived and swollen by the anti-semitism of the Right and the anti-militarism of the Left.

'The Dreyfus Affair,' Anatole France wrote, 'rendered an inestimable service to the country by bringing out and little by little revealing the forces of the past and the forces of the future: on the one side bourgeois authoritarianism and Catholic theocracy; on the other side socialism and free thought.' An anti-dreyfusard would have worded the summing up differently; he would have seen the forces of order and tradition aligned against the forces of disorder and revolution. But from whichever side the situation was defined one fact remained clear beyond doubt. France was more deeply divided than at any moment in the nineteenth century. The split in the French tradition seemed irremediable, and there were only two possible ends to the struggle: the extermination of one or the other side, or a stalemate that was bound to be sterile. Neither compromise nor reconciliation was in the vocabulary of either party.

The Dreyfus Affair quickly developed into a civil war between rival ideologies, and revealed the weakness and exhaustion of both sides who returned to the ideas of the past, which offered no hope of escape. The absurdly consistent anti-clericalism of Combes, who refused while Président du Conseil to entertain any project which did not directly forward his single desire to eliminate the Church in France, was countered by the insanely consistent political Catholicism of Charles Maurras. Combes, who was educated for the priesthood, led the anti-Clericals; Maurras, a declared atheist, the clerical Right. The war of 1914 and *l'union sacrée* were really the end of nineteenth century anti-clericalism and after 1918 it was in effect a spent force. But the grouping of the Right under Charles Maurras survived a few years longer, and its end was to coincide with the discovery of Péguy and the importance of his work.

The condemnation of Maurras's *Action Française* in 1926 marks the end of the political Catholicism which had thrived in France during the nineteenth century. A majority of the episcopate and of the higher clergy, as well as many of the influential Catholics among the laity, were deeply committed to the doctrines of Maurras. Their reaction to the condemnation in 1926 can be gauged from the fact that Cardinal Billot took the unprecedented step of

32,758

resigning the cardinalate in order to demonstrate his opposition to the Vatican policy.

Maurras's work had in fact been under examination in
Rome since 1907, but political considerations led Merry del
Val and the Pope to postpone the condemnation. When
Pius XI decided to re-open the case, at the instigation of
Cardinal Mercier, the files were not to be found, and he
undertook to study the books himself. The ground on
which he condemned them and the paper, *L'Action Française*, emerge in the interview which he gave at the time to
Henri Bordeaux. 'Maurras,' the Pope said, 'is one of the
fine brains of the present time; nobody knows him better
than I do. But he is only a brain . . . Reason does not
suffice.' Henri Bordeaux, who had gone to Rome to support the *Action Française*, recalled that Maurras was not the
only unbeliever to defend the Church in recent years and
mentioned the names of Taine, Bourget and Barrès.
'With the possible [*sic*] exception of Bourget,' the Pope
replied, 'they are all without faith . . . But what am I to
say to a young man who argues: why should I go further
than M. Maurras? You yourself recognise the force of his
logic; should that not suffice? Logic,' the Pope added,
'makes neither nations nor men.' Bordeaux pleaded that
Maurras simply put *la politique d'abord*—that was the
Action Française slogan—'because politics must protect
religion.' 'The opposite is true,' Pius concluded, 'it is
religion which protects politics.'

That was not a reversal of policy, such as Lamennais had
desired, but a call for a re-orientation of thought such as
Péguy inaugurated. By and large the nineteenth century
Catholics had thought and acted on the principle, *la
politique d'abord*, to the exclusion even of social questions.
The grounds which led the Pope to condemn the *Action*

Française, and in doing so the attitude of the Catholics in France, were the grounds which led Péguy to treat the clericals and anti-clericals as ultimately committed to the same ideas and to break with both. It was primarily the 'atmosphere' of the *Action Française* which the Pope censured, and in the new atmosphere which began to prevail after the condemnation, Péguy's work began to be understood.

The conception of tradition and freedom which that political attitude of mind had engendered in the nineteenth century meant in fact that freedom and tradition were opposed. The French tradition appeared therefore to have been split from top to bottom at the Revolution and the Dreyfus Affair simply aligned the two sides in the struggle, those who desired to return to tradition, to the past, and those who desired to continue the Revolution and the fight for freedom. Catholicism belonged to the past, and the future to those who believed in freedom.

IV

THE FOUNDATION OF THE *CAHIERS*

The *Cahiers* originated in the disagreement which broke out between Péguy and the Socialist leaders: Herr, the Librarian of the Sorbonne, Léon Blum, the future Prime Minister, Jaurès, the voice of the party, and others. Péguy imagined that his part in the Socialist Movement was to run a sort of Socialist Book Club, and act as typographer, publisher and publicist to the party that had joined issue with the Conservatives over the court-martial of Alfred Dreyfus. The undertaking was short-lived. Of the few books published only Jaurès's collected articles sold, though not sufficiently to cover the expenses of the optimistic printing. Within little more than a year the 'Librairie Georges Bellais' was on the rocks.

Péguy consulted Herr, who with Blum, Simiand, the sociologist, and two others, came without hesitation to his rescue. Péguy, they thought, was worth saving and could be an asset to the party. The committee of five bought him out, gave him some shares and retained financial control. They imagined that with money and position they could dictate the policy. By September 1899 the Dreyfus trial was over. Dreyfus was at liberty, Waldeck-Rousseau had replaced Méline, and the Socialists had gained an overwhelming victory that was to be demonstrated at the polls in 1902. The trouble with Péguy arose as Waldeck-Rousseau began to exploit his gains, and the Socialists supporting him consolidated their position and their power.

In September 1899 Herr and Blum were astonished to

read an article by Péguy in the *Revue Blanche* in which he criticised Guesde, the Marxist, who had built up the Unions in the north and represented the trade union section of the party. Guesde, they read, knew no more about Socialism than Leo XIII about Christianity at the time of the Armenian massacres—on which subject he had not satisfied Péguy. The statement shocked them and the parallel suggested a detachment of mind they were not prepared to tolerate. If anything was sacred it was the fundamental difference between Socialism and Catholicism. Péguy was called to order by his directors. '*Pardon, monsieur,*' he makes his *citoyen libre* say in the *Réponse Provisoire*: 'I only wanted to know what persons are to exert the impersonal dictatorship of the working class.' His article, *Le Triomphe de la République*, which appeared later as a *Cahier*, was refused by Lagardelle, at the instigation, Péguy presumed, of Herr. To settle the matter he informed his directors that he proposed publishing a fortnightly news bulletin dealing with the progress of the 'revolution'. The five had begun to see what Péguy meant by news, and they had no intention of subsidising uncut and unvarnished accounts of their congresses. Blum looked coldly at him through his pince-nez and described the proposal as inopportune. Simiand was contemptuous: 'Je vois ce que c'est: tu veux faire une revue pour les imbéciles.' Herr gave the practical conclusion. He informed Péguy that they were all agreed in thinking that he had turned against them. 'You are an anarchist,' he ended, 'and we shall oppose you with all our might.' Péguy was thunderstruck.

His position was critical. He had a wife and child to support and most of their capital had been lost. He was alone in a world where party backing was essential. He was dismayed, but unmoved in his decision. With the help of the Tharauds and the support of a few friends who had known him since the days of the *cour rose*, at the Collège Sainte-Barbe, he moved his headquarters into the Tharauds' rooms and put his plan into action. The fortnightly *Cahiers* began appearing, some of them being reports and comments on the political scene; others were written entirely by Péguy himself, and in addition he published anything that came his way, a play by Romain Rolland, a novel by the Tharauds, another volume by Jaurès.

We should have died of asphyxia (Rolland writes of the young men who supported Péguy) and of depression, but for the indomitable tenacity of Péguy, who ended by breaking down the resistance of a few hundred people, hardly any of them with any reputation or standing—and but for the occasional stroke of luck, such as the sudden stir caused by my little life of Beethoven . . . our success owed nothing to the world of letters.

The *Cahiers de la Quinzaine* were launched, and for the rest of his days Péguy was never out of harness.

Péguy's *Cahiers** from 1900 to 1908 are largely concerned with his gradual break with the Socialist Party. The constructive thought is often overlaid by the criticism, or set in such unexpected positions that its implications are far from clear. The two processes in fact go hand in hand. Péguy only slowly understood the character of his original intuition, and to unfold his argument took him thousands of pages. His Socialism, for one thing, was not skin-deep, and the break with Jaurès was neither brusque,

*The word *Cahier* includes, strictly speaking, everything published in the series. But Péguy's work is so thoroughly identified with the *Cahiers*, that no other term adequately describes his books.

nor did he desire it. Jaurès continued to treat his junior with respect and affection, and until 1902 there was forbearance on both sides.

In 1902 Jaurès was returned to Parliament after an absence of four years. He was elected Vice-President of the Chamber and for the next few years was at the height of his power. The Radicals, led by Combes who succeeded Waldeck-Rousseau, depended on the Socialist vote, and Jaurès gave them the rope to carry out their anti-clerical policy which they hoped might distract attention from the social revolution Jaurès stood for. An ideological victory over the Church might once again postpone a more tangible Socialist victory. Péguy regarded the agreement between them as the triumph of the wrong republic, and when Combes's anti-clerical policy got under way, he broke finally with Jaurès. The violence of his attacks on the Socialist leader is an expression of the bitterness of his disappointment. He had looked up to Jaurès as the man above all others who could have led France back to unity in a Socialist state, and now he only found him supporting the *ressentiment* of a spoilt priest, Combes, and the vindictive last stand of the old Radicals. Instead of unity he was offered *la politique à outrance*. The Two Nations were to be perpetuated. And as the anti-clerical policy extended through education and into the army, Péguy began to see the moral and military weakness of the country. Anti-militarism had not of course harmed the careers of the General Staff, responsible for the Dreyfus case, but it profoundly affected the morale of the army, and Péguy loved the army.

Notre Patrie (October 1905) marks a second phase in the *Cahiers* of this period. From then on Péguy was full of foreboding for the future. The defeat of Russia in the

Russo-Japanese War taught him to look more sceptically at Russian strength; the fall of Delcassé, who was largely responsible for the *Entente Cordiale*, and finally the Tangier incident, made him realise that France was not only weakened internally, but in danger of being once again isolated. The German menace redoubled his anger with the Socialists who took comfort in Jaurès's assurance that the Sozial Demokraten would never march against their French brothers. Péguy did not hesitate to call him a traitor. On all sides, at home and abroad, he saw *l'inondation barbare* submerging not only France but Europe, and the 'enormous belly' of material civilisation devouring its spirit. He had never felt so much alone, for he was almost alone in remaining true to the spirit of the Dreyfusards, and those who had fought at his side had simply used the victory of a just cause to perpetrate a great injustice.

During all these years the *Cahiers* were a continual source of anxiety. He had begun with 150 subscribers and his dogged determination had raised the subscription list to 1,100—but expenses were not always balanced by receipts. It was at about this time that Maritain came generously to his assistance. The *Cahiers* could be said to have had a *succès d'estime*. Jaurès, Poincaré, Doumergue, and a number of politicians subscribed. But apart from Faguet, Gide and Lanson, the literary and intellectual world showed little interest. Literature and politics were still different spheres, and that was among the causes of Péguy's difficulties. Romain Rolland and the Tharauds were already names. Péguy had no following but for a handful of friends. And considering no one knew where Péguy was going, it is hardly surprising.

Moreover, from any recognised standpoint Péguy was not going anywhere: he was still harping on the Dreyfus case, still digging down to the fundamental questions it set, so that when he came to look back on this period of his life in *Notre Jeunesse* (1910) he called the process not an evolution but an *approfondissement*. This accounts in part for the repetitions in his work, which, after allowing for much that is unnecessary, are not always repetitions but variations on a theme which at each *reprise* go deeper, and reveal a new aspect of the subject. The very nature of his *approfondissement* is what makes it so difficult to compress or select from the *Cahiers* without destroying their unity, the flow and consistency of what Rolland calls 'the great river of his prose'.

V

'NOTHING BUT THE TRUTH'

Le Triomphe de la République, dated January 1900, was written to celebrate the unveiling of a monument to the Republic, and confirmed Herr and Simiand in their view that Péguy was bent upon producing a review *pour les imbéciles*, a theoretical, unpractical Socialism for idealists. 'The revolution,' Péguy announced, 'will be moral, or there will not be any.' And he proceeded to assert his principle and his method:

'To tell the truth, the whole truth and nothing but the truth, to tell the stupid truth stupidly, the dull truth dully and the sad truth sadly: that is what we propose to do . . .'

This was asking for failure, and Péguy lived up to his words; he was always frank, sometimes dull, often sad. Very few of his readers could see where such a pure idealism could rejoin practical questions. Where everyone else was arguing *what* should be done, Péguy took an unconscionable time reflecting on *how* anything should be done. The Socialists were in power, they knew what they wanted, and meant to get it. They could not see why Péguy should be touchy about their methods, their alliance with Combes, their use of anti-clericalism.

Péguy's first steps bear a certain similarity to Kierkegaard's, whose earliest articles were an attack on the Liberal Party which was just taking shape in Denmark. The Liberals could not understand what he was at; for as his biographer, Fritjof Brandt, observes, when a Socratic mind interferes in a political situation, the man who intervenes seems to the crowd to be talking at cross-purposes. What could a moral revolution mean to those in power? They were talking about policies; Péguy was talking about words:

'One cannot be seriously converted to Socialism unless one's philosophy and life and one's deepest feelings are renewed, refreshed and, to keep the word, converted.'

He had kept the word salvation, in *Jeanne d'Arc*, and now he kept the word converted. That was the danger of moral revolutions. Had Péguy shown any signs of changing sides, of joining the Clerical, Conservative Party, his attitude would have been intelligible. Instead, he made his opposition quite clear: *Je m'attaquerai donc à la foi chrétienne.* He had no more desire to side with the Right than with the Left: the more he considered them, the more they came to resemble one another. Both sides believed in power and wanted it. Unity, in their eyes, meant power— not the 'city' as he was to say, but the 'state'.

This is the question Péguy turns to in the *Cahiers* for February, March and April of the year 1900: *De la Grippe*, *Encore de la Grippe* and *Toujours de la Grippe*, written, as the titles indicate, during a bout of influenza.

While in bed, Péguy had been reading Pascal's *Prière pour le bon usage des maladies* at Tharaud's suggestion, but before he got very far he was interrupted by a visit from *le docteur moraliste révolutionnaire* (half Péguy, half Georges Sorel, I suspect), and the humorous, ironical dialogue that meanders through the three *Cahiers* begins. What he had to say was summed up in the *Réponse brève à Jaurès*:

You firmly believe that unity is the condition of everything, that one must construct unity before all else, and that everything will follow from unity. You expect nothing of duality and plurality except the victorious tyranny of the one and the servitude of the other, or the neutralisation of both in the vacuum of a sterile equilibrium.

How Péguy applied his argument to both sides in the struggle can be seen from the illustration which he gives: 'Once the idea of Catholic unity has entered the soul of a monk, and once the idea of Socialist unity has entered the soul of a *citoyen*, those men become unrecognisable.'

It is hardly surprising that neither the clericals nor the anti-clericals understood Péguy's argument, but when Romain Rolland fails to perceive his drift we can begin to gauge the originality of his position. Like many others Rolland sees Péguy attacking the very idea of unity, not only at war with the unity Jaurès meant to impose, and the unity the Catholics hoped to impose, but with unity itself. Lucien Herr, Rolland is inclined to think, was not far wrong when he used the word anarchist, and he himself repeats the charge in gentler terms, calling Péguy 'the free man, absolutely free, free even from the illusion of unity . . . the man who feels no need to unify the world.' And having failed to understand what Péguy was talking about he runs on in the same vein to speak of 'that diseased passion for liberty which is Péguy's very soul'. Coming from Rolland who always thought of himself as standing *au-dessus de la mêlée*—even in 1914—the expression *passion maladive de la liberté* carries its full weight and though the sense in which he describes Péguy as the absolutely free man is utterly false it has the merit of emphasising the strength of Péguy's faith in freedom.

There is no moment in Péguy's life when he could be called an anarchist, except to emphasise his hatred of enforced unity. Far from rejecting unity, Péguy's whole work might be described as the pursuit of unity through freedom, and of unity as the fruit of freedom. That is the system which he afterwards called 'a system of courage', of faith which brought unity in its train. This he first saw in the Dreyfus case, as the fundamental difference between himself and Jaurès and Maurras. Jaurès believed that unity was the starting point, the condition of action and achievement. In this, Péguy points out, he was adopting the political outlook of his opponents, and to say that unity comes first is to say *la politique d'abord*.* It meant thinking in terms of politics, which is to say in terms of power.

One must never forget (he wrote subsequently, in *Notre Jeunesse* [1910]) that Combisme, the Combes system, the Combes tyranny, the source of all our ills, was the invention of Jaurès with his detestable political power, his oratorical power, his parliamentary power, who imposed that invention, that tyranny, on the country.

It was not until *Notre Jeunesse*, one of the great *Cahiers*, that Péguy elaborated his conception of unity and explained why his opponents were committed to power politics. Neither party, he holds, believed in freedom; at the most they wanted certain liberties for themselves. Their *politiques* were divorced from any *mystique*, and when that happens the end ultimately justifies the means. But Rolland does not appear to have understood what Péguy meant by a *mystique*, and is consequently left to conclude that because Péguy attacked the unity in which Jaurès believed he denied all forms of unity. And yet Péguy's meaning is clear enough. He held that unity in the true sense is the fruit of a spiritual attitude, of faith which is itself free, and

*He also accused the *Action Française* much later of being false to its principles when it adopted the Socialist tactics of causing disturbances.

that a mystique or faith confers life, morality and consistency upon its *politique*, upon the action which flows from
a *mystique*. But a *politique* which has become divorced from
its *mystique* ceases to be alive, it ceases to be unity and tends
to become uniformity, and as power comes to replace
faith as the source of action, unity becomes the contrary of
freedom. For that reason all *politiques* divorced from their
mystique tend to resemble one another.

The full implications of Péguy's conception of freedom
and unity were only developed subsequently, after his
conversion, which was itself the concrete and complete
expression of his *fidélité* to the past, to his original intuition
and belief in freedom. For the moment he retained the
word conversion, just as in the first *Jeanne d'Arc* and *La
cité harmonieuse* he retained the word salvation—though
emphasising only its temporal meaning, and even rejecting
its eternal sense. But as he pondered on the case of Jaurès,
and then of Renan, whose influence was still paramount, he
began to use the word conversion in a special sense, applying it to those who, like Renan, had changed sides.

Why, he asks, does Jaurès bind himself to 'the inextric-
able pell-mell and amalgam of metaphysical, Socialist,
materialist unity—a sort of lay providence which he sub-
stitutes for religious providence'? And at this point, in *De
la Grippe,* he begins the prolonged criticism of Renan
whose historicism and naturalism he came to regard as the
philosophy of *le monde moderne*, the world from which the
very idea of the sacred had been excluded. Renan, he says
in *Zangwill* (1904), simply changed sides and abandoned
one hypothesis for another, for the more difficult and less
clear hypothesis of progress and a naïve belief in science.
Moreover, Renan had imported a vaguely religious atmosphere into his new world. 'Don't let's be religious,' he con-

cludes, 'even with Renan,' though he was not insensitive
to the charm of the old sophist. 'In truth, Renan could
make one fall in love with pedantry.' But he had no time
for the elegant reveries with which Renan concealed his
scientific naturalism and an innate pessimism. 'I haven't
the time. I work by the fortnight. I cling to the present.'
Neither Renan's charm nor the great voice of Jaurès could
keep him from the work of *approfondissement* that was
going on in the *Cahiers*.

Yet neither then nor later did Péguy have any illusions
about the Catholic Party. If he refused to admit that he
abandoned his Socialism, he also refused to admit that he
was converted from Socialism to the Catholic Party:

It cannot be denied that there was infinitely more Christianity
in our Socialism (not Jaurès's) than in the whole of the Madeleine
together with Saint-Pierre-de-Chaillot and Saint-Phillipe-du-
Roule and Saint-Honoré-d'Eylau. It was essentially a religion of
temporal poverty. We shall be marked by it for the whole of our
temporal lives, and for the next too . . . It is a sort of vocation
. . . All the forces of the Church were against Dreyfusism. The
political forces of the Church have always been against *la mystique*.
Particularly against the Christian *mystique* . . . Our Christianity
will never be a parliamentary Christianity, nor the Christianity of
a rich parish . . . (The Church) is the official religion, the formal
religion of the rich. That is what the poor very certainly feel,
obscurely or explicitly.

The *Cahiers* were gradually moving deeper, further
away from conformist Socialism and conformist Catholicism. For much of the time Péguy could only define his
position in relation to the two parties he refused to recognise, until at first indistinctly, and finally quite clearly, it
was borne in upon him that he stood at the centre.

'Péguy,' Albert Béguin writes, 'was the only or almost the only man of our period who saw the unity of France in time'—who did not regard the Revolution as a break in the historical continuity of France. The conclusions which he had drawn from the Dreyfus Affair were diametrically opposed to those of Anatole France and Charles Maurras. The Dreyfus Affair had begun by confusing his intuition, but in the debates and disputes that followed he was obliged to clarify his thought. The unity of France in time was not an ideology but his heritage. He was born in Orleans and came of a peasant stock that had very different feelings from the men of the Sorbonne. His first two books, *Jeanne d'Arc* and *De la cité harmonieuse,* were two aspects of that unity, even though at first he might not see clearly how they were one. The Clericals and the anti-Clericals represented contraries, but that was not at all the same thing as saying that the faith of Jeanne was opposed to the faith of the *cité harmonieuse*. At the root of each was a certain *fidélité*, a faith and a courage which Clerical and anti-Clerical lacked.

And yet he did not think that the existing divisions could be healed by compromise, a new policy or a shift of alliances. His thought moves in the opposite direction from Lamennais's, who wished to begin with unity. Logic, he knew, could not build nations or men, and reason was not enough. The central intuition which was to co-ordinate his at first sight paradoxical thought was still lacking, and it was the release of his imagination, the birth of his poetry, that supplied him with the key to the unity of tradition and freedom, the unity of faith which showed him the unity of France in time.

If Socialism could only be understood as the result of a conversion, the same was true of Catholicism. The *Cahiers* down to 1907 had led him as far as they could. They had begun in an ironical, almost bantering tone which steadily darkened as the texture of his thought became closer. At first there are echoes of Anatole France, touches of Sorel, until Péguy alone is speaking.

'But the real Anatole France,' Rolland writes, 'is affected, *faux-bonhomme*, compared with Péguy, in whom everything is frank and everything first hand. Even when he imitates or remembers, Péguy remains Péguy—whose like will not be seen again—and then beneath the irony of his rich dialogues, what a genuine seriousness . . .

'One by one, I turned the pages of that long monologue, which goes on its way, bifurcating into side-paths and dwelling on some astonishing discoveries, and in the end, at the very end, regaining the high-road . . . The most striking thing—the thing which so often touches one to the quick, is the unique tone of confession, complete, total, entire, surpassing in depths any which has ever been heard —particularly in the last *Cahiers*—where it gives up the tragic secrets of the man—neither Jean-Jacques, nor Tolstoy even, dared avow themselves to that extent.'

But Péguy's confession does not surpass Rousseau's or Tolstoy's: it is of a different order. He is like the pilgrim in his *Holy Innocents*; he does not 'go on wiping his boots on the threshold', he enters the Church. Confession for Péguy is always at the point at which it merges into confession of faith. He leaves his sins and his private world behind him so that nothing remains but his personal faith. The *Cahiers* may begin as confessions, but the moment came when they became a confession of faith, the growth of *l'âme paienne* into *l'âme chrétienne*. The *Cahiers* themselves continue without interruption, but Péguy himself published nothing after the autumn of 1907. And except for a short

Cahier on the material difficulties the *Cahiers* were encountering, his next contribution was *The Mystery of the Charity of Joan of Arc*, in which it was revealed that Péguy was a Catholic and a poet.

VI

THE PROCESS OF *APPROFONDISSEMENT*

In September 1908 Joseph Lotte, Professor at the Lycée at Coutances, and one of the friends whom Péguy had known since the days of the *cour rose*, arrived in Paris, and finding that Péguy was in bed with influenza, went out to visit him. 'I have not told you everything,' Péguy said, by way of introducing the subject. 'I have become a Catholic again.' Lotte answered: 'We're all in the same boat then.'

More than a year earlier, Péguy had confided the secret of his return to the Church to Maritain who was authorised to inform Dom Baillet, one of Péguy's old friends, a Benedictine. The community to which he belonged had been obliged by the Combes laws to leave France, and had settled in England. Madame Favre, Maritain's mother, was not to be told. But Péguy did tell her, without warning Maritain, and this produced the first of a series of misunderstandings. Moreover, Péguy, who regarded Bloy as a 'fanatic', probably resented his influence on Maritain.

One reason for Péguy's secrecy is that his conversion had created a very difficult family situation. Neither his wife nor his mother-in-law could understand his conversion and, as the Maritains themselves had found, anyone who joined the Church was regarded as a traitor to 'progress', and in the case of the Baudouins, to Socialism. The strength of feeling shown astonished Maritain when, at Péguy's request, he went to discuss the situation. The difficulties far surpassed anything he had imagined and he has since, as Madame Maritain writes in *Les Grandes Amitiés*,

reproached himself for having taken his rôle as 'ambas-
sador' too literally, and for pressing arguments on Péguy
instead of trusting in providence. Péguy was not indeed
what most people expected a convert to be, and Georges
Sorel, an unbeliever, doubted his return to the Church
until 1914.

But Péguy did not tell everyone everything, and it is
impossible to say exactly when he returned to the Church
except that his words to Lotte, his confidant, mark a
decisive moment. Moreover, there was no sudden change
of sides to note, no change of opinions to record. The process which he calls an *approfondissement* reaches back to his
earliest years, for it was not a change but a growth. The
culmination of the *approfondissement* was the coming of
grace: 'One must be suspicious of grace,' he makes Clio
say, 'when it wants a creature it gets him. It does not take
the path we take. It does not even follow its own paths. It
never takes the same path twice. Grace is perhaps free,'
Clio concludes, 'grace which is the source of all freedom.'
Neither recent converts nor unbelievers were prepared to
think that grace was as free as Péguy maintained.

On the few occasions when he refers to the event, Péguy
spoke of his 'return to Catholicism' and refused to admit
that he had been 'converted'. He had not journeyed in the
opposite direction to Renan. And unless his distinction is
admitted the nature of his *approfondissement* cannot be fully
understood. There is, of course, a sense in which his views
changed. But he objected to the word conversion because
it both minimised the metamorphosis and exaggerated the
change. It implied that the change in *his* opinion was the
important point, when it was his path that mattered; it
suggested that it was an interesting event in his private life.
To him it was neither a break with the past nor a return to

the past nor even an evolution. Péguy felt that the freedom and continuity of the growth had involved a complete transformation: a renewal, the continuation of the renewal of his feelings and thoughts with which he identified his Socialism.

We have always carried on in the same direction (he wrote in 1911, using the editorial 'we' of the *Cahiers*), we stuck to the same straight path, the self-same path that led us to where we now stand . . . It was by a continual deepening of the heart along the same path, and not as the result of an 'evolution', in no sense by retracing our steps, that we found the Christian path. We did not find it by turning back. We found it at the end. That is why we shall never deny our path. We may have been sinners. We certainly were; very much so. *Pro nobis peccatoribus*. But we never ceased to be on the right path. Our invincible fidelity, our youthful fidelity to Christian morals, to Christian poverty, to the deepest lessons of the Gospels, our obstinate, our altogether natural fidelity, moving secretly within us, constitute an invisible parish.

That deepening of the heart, that secret and consistent growth is like a tradition which does not remain sterile but culminates in something new: a revolution. At first he had said the revolution must be moral, adding that one could not be seriously converted to Socialism unless one's philosophy of life was renewed and one's deepest feelings refreshed. He had kept the word converted. But when the event followed the word proved inadequate to the reality. 'A revolution is not an operation whereby one contradicts oneself. It is an operation whereby one renews oneself and becomes new. That is in part why there are so few revolutions in the modern world.'

A revolution in Péguy's sense was not a break with

tradition, or the reverse of tradition: it was a renaissance, an expression of the vitality of tradition, a path leading into the Christian path, not a dead-end. Only a moribund tradition which has ceased to be free and lazily relies on the past loses the capacity (and freedom) to renew itself from within, without denying the past. Then it ceases to create new forms and takes refuge in a Byzantine formula, in which the letter hermetically seals down the spirit.

But the real nature of his *approfondissement* was revealed to Péguy and to his friends neither by his explanations nor by their criticism, but by a fact. Even those who regarded Péguy's *Cahiers* up to this time as eccentric in their refusal to take sides, and those who recognised the virtue of his unrepentant idealism, were brought up short and compelled to attend when, at the age of thirty-five, Péguy embarked on a series of poems which revealed the transformation which had taken place. He is, I believe, the only poet of importance who began writing in middle life and towards the close of his work. In retrospect it is of course possible to find analogies in the prose *Cahiers* for the poetry which grew out of them. But to his friends and those who followed the *Cahiers* his poetry came unheralded, and his genius exploded without warning. It was then that the deepest note in Péguy's spiritual constitution, what Romain Rolland called his diseased love of liberty, became articulate and the revolution in his own life taught him the revolutionary note in Christianity which his contemporaries for the most part feared or forgot. In one sense, no doubt, his prose is freer than his verse: it takes greater liberties with the rules of prosody, but his freedom is limited by the liberties he took, and his idiosyncrasies can be very tiresome. His poetry is more completely free, because its form expresses that freedom. The more powerful the inspiration, the more complete the form and unity of the work.

The metamorphosis was complete when the relation between freedom and form which Péguy had been groping towards was illustrated in his poetry. What Péguy discovered in his own way, was not something unheard of, but a new and fruitful understanding of the relation between freedom and truth. A classic instance of the same discovery is the renewal of Pascal's style as a result of his conversion. In one of his letters Pascal discussed the question in terms which provide an instructive introduction to Péguy's own account of the same double event.

Your zeal (Pascal writes to Mademoiselle de Roannez) is altogether new to me; it is that new language that a new heart ordinarily produces. In the Gospels, Jesus Christ has given this sign by which to recognise those who have faith, which is that they will talk a new language, and, in effect, the renewal of our thoughts and desires causes that of our discourse . . . The truths of Christianity (he continues) are certainly new things, but they must be renewed continually; for this newness which cannot be displeasing to God, any more than the old man can please him, is different from the newness of the world, in that the things of the world, however new they may be, grow old as they endure; whereas the new spirit continues to renew itself increasingly as it endures. The old man perishes, St. Paul says, and is renewed from day to day, and will only be perfect in eternity where the New Canticle, of which David speaks in the Psalm at Laudes, will be sung, that is to say, the Canticle which springs from the new spirit of charity.

In the last section of *The Holy Innocents* Péguy develops his theme in almost the same way, emphasising still more, if possible, the creative character of the innocent heart.

A tous les autres témoins, à tous ces autres martyrs il ne fut pas
*   donné . . .*
Eternellement il n'est pas donné de chanter ce cantique nouveau.
Et attention, ils ne chantaient pas seulement un cantique
Mais il chantaient un cantique nouveau devant le siège.
C'est un cantique nouveau pour marquer
Cette éternelle nouveauté qu'il y a dans l'enfance.
Et qui est le grand secret de ma grâce.
Cette renaissante, cette perpétuellement renaissante, cette éternelle-
*   ment renaissante nouveauté.*

It was not a matter of words for Péguy to say that he was
not converted. Nowhere in his work, as far as I can re-
member, does he speak of his conversion as an experience,
not because he did not wish to talk about his deepest experiences, but because he never saw his life in that light.
He had no sense of having changed. There is only one
description of the coming of grace, and that is indirect, in
the *Commentary on Eve* when he describes the new language which proceeded from the renewal of his deepest
feelings.

VII

THE COMMENTARY ON *EVE*

Until Béguin published the full text of the *Commentary* in *L'Eve de Péguy* it received little or no attention. Romain Rolland, for example, makes no real use of it, for although he tries to avoid defining Péguy's return to Catholicism as a conversion, recognising the justice of Péguy's objection to the word, he does not understand the implications of Péguy's new sense of liberty. He is driven in the end to regard him as *sui generis*. By doing so he fails to bring out the originality of Péguy's conception of the unity of freedom and tradition. He is compelled to juggle with his own concepts and to reconcile as best he can Péguy's 'diseased love of freedom' and his acceptance of Catholic unity. For as long as Péguy's 'conversion' is presented primarily as a change in him, as an 'evolution' and not as the fruit of freedom and grace bringing with it a new vision, the essence of his attitude remains hidden.

Eve, Péguy's epic, is the mature expression of his return to Catholicism. It is both 'what happened to him' and what he sees, and is the culmination of his whole work, so that it provides the framework in which to understand how he came to see it. The *Commentary*, for all its exaggerations and oddities (and there are plenty of them), remains the most important document for the understanding of his *approfondissement*, since even the expression 'return' throws the emphasis back on to Péguy, whereas the whole stress should fall not on *his* return to the faith, but on faith itself.

P.—D

It is clear enough (Béguin writes) that Péguy's first concern in dictating, writing and recasting the *Commentary* was to mark the profound unity of his work; not only of *Eve*, which constitutes his great Christian vision of human history, but of everything he wrote. It is an *art poétique*, and like that of all great poets—Claudel's, for example—is much more than a personal aesthetic. *Eve* is the poem of the universe, of creation unfolding and revealing its secret around the mystery of nature and grace. Such is the form, the architecture of the centuries in time, linked to eternity, which inspires Péguy as he builds his *oeuvre*.

In the *Commentary* Péguy turns to the question of the renewal of language which sprang directly from the renewal of his faith. And in it he defines the relation between the two.

One may say that in *Eve* (and for *Eve* read the process of *approfondissement*) Péguy succeeded in descending to that spiritual depth whence everything subsequently rises up again according to different modes, and manifests itself according to will, as it were, in liturgy, in theology, in history . . .

In the same way that Péguy descended, in the matter of faith, to the depths where liturgy and theology, that is to say, the spiritual life and the spiritual proposition are as yet undifferentiated, so too as a writer he redescended in this work to the depths where the image and the idea are still joined by a liaison which is itself carnal and not yet resolved.

His *approfondissement*, the deepening of the heart of which he speaks elsewhere, and which is now described as a descent to the point at which inspiration and form are as yet undifferentiated, is not the confusion but the fusion of thought and feeling, so lucid that it becomes articulate. It is only then that the whole man can speak and so discovers a 'new language' in order to communicate all that he now sees. I shall return to consider in further detail what Péguy implied by this descent to the depths, but for the moment follow the text of the *Commentary* which goes straight on to speak of the style which he requires to express all he sees:

There is no trace of *placage*, never the impression of an image coming after, or to the rescue [of the idea]; image and idea spring up together from the same fecundity. It was particularly necessary in a work whose subject is the mysterious liaison of the carnal and the spiritual, that the carnal and spiritual of thought should not be any more distinct than the carnal and spiritual of faith.

The poems which followed immediately on Péguy's return to Catholicism are its direct expression. They are not *about* his faith and still less about his return to the faith. They are the incarnation and communication of his faith and of the grace and contemplation given to him. But in the *Commentary* his mind races on to a further definition of the newly found unity which he was to expand and illustrate in the last great *Cahier*, the *Note Conjointe*.

One of the immediate results is the disappearance of any arbitrary separation of abstract and concrete. The abstract is immediately nourished by the concrete, and the concrete illuminated continually by the abstract. This result dismisses the claims of both intellectualists and intuitionists, both of whom are more concerned to deny than to produce.

Here Péguy is once again asserting that he had not been 'converted', that he had not changed sides philosophically and that he had not abandoned the intellectualism of his youth for a confused intuitionism, the confusion attributed by the intellectuals to Bergson. He does not allow that the world is divided into rationalists and irrationalists. Throughout the *Commentary* he is pursuing the same task which made the *Cahiers* incomprehensible to his contemporaries, digging down towards the centre and rejecting the one-sided extremes into which his contemporaries fell.

'*Eve*,' he then says, 'is equally opposed, equally contrary to the fecundities of disorder and the sterilities of order', as far from the sterile orderliness of an effete classicism as from the disorderly profusion of a decadent romanticism. The context makes it clear that Péguy was not thinking solely of literary schools and *genres*, but of the mental climate of the period which contrasted order and disorder in such a way that tradition and revolution appeared as contraries.

At this point Péguy's Catholicism can be seen emerging from the depth of his *approfondissement* taking shape with the inevitability of a vision suddenly clarified. For after saying that *Eve* is equally contrary to the sterilities of order and the fecundities of disorder he goes on at once to ask whether this central position is not Catholicity: 'Is that not Catholicism itself, and Catholicity? Is that not the situation . . . of Catholicity within the generality of Christendom? All the forces of creation, all the resources of nature and grace gathered together and harvested at the feet of God.'

That is Péguy's definition of Catholicity, as the fertile union of freedom and tradition. He did not have any sense of being 'converted' to it, but of having remained at the centre where he had always been, till he finally saw Catholicity defined not by its circumference, which is changing, but by its spiritual centre, by the grace and freedom which define its unity as the inspiration of a poem dictates its form.

The new element in Péguy's definition consists in the *movement* and direction of his thought. He does not start from unity, but from fecundity. Freedom and grace are not perceived in the form alone but in the relation between the freedom, the fecundity and the form they create. The centre or spirit orders the circumference. This is expressed in the *Commentary* in the opening passage on *le jaillissement*. 'Tout le jaillissement dans le germe, tout l'ordre dans l'épi.'—'All the fecundity is in the seed, all the order in the fruit.' Is that not Catholicism, he asks, the Christianity which created Christendom?

To look at Catholicism the other way round, not merely from the circumference, but at the circumference, at its institutional unity, is not to see it all, and to misinterpret everything. Those who do so may admire the structure or dislike the unity; almost certainly they deny its freedom, which is to say its life, and by implication its faith. That was the 'incredible confusion', the 'incredible abuse of language' which astonished and dismayed Péguy. For he writes:

Liberty consists in believing. And in admitting that the other man believes . . . Liberty is a system of courage . . . And another word I don't like, but after all *life* itself demands liberty . . . I love nothing so much as liberty. And in itself is it not the irrevocable condition of grace?

To be free, Péguy says, is to believe. To assert that one's adversary is not free is to deny his faith and equate it with superstition. That, he says, is cheating. 'Here (in the *Cahiers*) we are Catholics who don't cheat; Protestants who don't cheat; Jews who don't cheat; Free-thinkers who don't cheat. Altogether very few.' Against him are all those who cheat: Lavisse the free-thinker, Laudet the

Catholic and the rest. 'And that makes a lot of people.' The source of the unity of the *Cahiers* was their liberty.

But Péguy may appear to be retreating behind words: fecundity is liberty, liberty is faith. And as can be seen from his dislike of the word *life*, he was alive to the danger that he would be thought to be advocating some form of vitalism. Once again he was in opposition to those who wished to judge and measure everything with the compass of their two-pronged antithesis. He offered no system of philosophy but a system of courage, by which he meant the courage to believe that freedom was not the road to disorder and revolution but the seed of tradition and the root of unity. He remained equally opposed to the intellectualists and the intuitionists, to the 'clear ideas' of the rationalist, and the 'confused emotion' of the intuitionist. 'All philosophies,' he writes in the *Note Conjointe*, 'are obviously and evidently rational. Even a philosophy which was or purported to be against reason, would still be rationalist.' But 'The real business of the philosopher is to see.' And the first thing which Péguy sees in the *Note Conjointe* is the danger of reducing man to a 'rational animal', a creature with only one faculty, reason.

The idea that the pathetic [the realm of feeling] is an inferior realm must be abandoned. It is like the others and as in Molière: it is inferior when it is inferior, and it is not inferior when it is not inferior. It is not an exception to the general rule governing levels. It is not inferior because it is pathetic. It is inferior when it is of poor quality, of low extraction . . . No one will ever make me say that comedy is an inferior form. As for tragedy, I confess that I would give the three *Critiques* (Kant is the subject of the opening of the *Note Conjointe*) preceded by half a hundredweight of Prolegomenas, for a chorus from the *Antigone*. And by that I do not mean that I would give them in respect of beauty, which is obvious, *sub specie pulchri*, but that I would give them, no less in respect of truth, in respect of reality, *sub specie res ac realitas*. And that there is infinitely more, an infinitely different, knowledge in that pathos than in the *Critiques*, a deepening of nature, of man and of fate.

The man of whom Péguy is speaking is not the rational animal of the *philosophes* of all times, but the complete man, created in the image of God, whose freedom is expressed in his faith and who serves God as God wishes to be served:

> *Librement*
> *Gratuitement,*
> *Par de vrais hommes, virils, adultes, fermes,*
> *Nobles, tendres, d'une tendresse ferme.*
> *Pour obtenir cette liberté (dit Dieu) j'ai tout sacrifié*
> *Pour obtenir cette liberté, cette gratuité*
> *Pour faire jouer cette liberté, cette gratuité*
> *Pour lui apprendre cette liberté.*

Not only reason and will but memory, perhaps above all memory, must be present to produce *de vrais hommes*: *Or c'est la mémoire qui fait toute la profondeur de l'homme . . . La mémoire s'enfonce et plonge et sonde dans l'événement.*

When Péguy speaks of descending to the depths where image and idea are still one, where the spiritual life and the spiritual proposition are as yet indistinguishable, and where pathos and reason are still united, he is searching for images to describe the fullness of decision which Pascal expressed in his most famous phrase, 'the reasons of the heart'. What Pascal meant has hardly been better stated than by Sainte-Beuve: 'Pascal,' he says, '*ne scinde pas l'homme.*'

'He does not divide man up; he does not set reason apart,

sensibility on another side, will on yet another; he does not work to make such and such a faculty operate.'

Pascal's endeavour is to find a way of allowing the complete man to give all his reasons, to use all his knowledge, to use not only reason, but will, feeling and memory. Sainte-Beuve's way of stating the harmony of a mature nature first occurs when he tried to analyse the spell which Lamennais cast upon him at the time. He ascribes that authority to the 'unity of reason, feeling and will which is called faith'. Subsequently, when he discovered his mistake and saw through Lamennais, he applied the same formula to Pascal. But 'the reasons of the heart', as Pascal had discovered, could only be formulated in a new language, because the heart itself could only speak if it were renewed.

Péguy had found 'the Christian path' by a continual deepening of the heart, not by 'turning back' and rejecting the truth on which his whole life had been built, but by enlarging his vision. 'That is why we shall never deny our path.' His natural faith, his good faith, all that he means by the word *fidélité* was open to reality. He did not find the Christian path by rejecting the modern world but sticking to the path which had taught him a profound respect for everything human.

It is often a pagan soul [Clio says, in the *Dialogue de l'âme paienne*] that makes the best Christian soul . . . That after all must be so, for in actual fact (*historically*, she said) the Christian soul was made out of a pagan soul, and not out of nothing. The Christian world was made out of the pagan world, and not out of nothing. The Christian city was made out of the city of antiquity, and in no sense out of nothing (out of a *zéro de cité*). These moderns lack soul. But they are the first to do so. The world of antiquity did not lack soul . . . It is not a matter of defending their Gods. They are indefensible . . . But what you will have to ask yourself, among other things [Clio continues], is whether the religion of Olympus was really the religion of the world of antiquity.

There was, Clio goes on to suggest, an element of contempt, perhaps rooted in envy, in the attitude of the Greeks towards the Gods. An element of contempt because:

[they] lacked the triple grandeur of man, death, misery and risk. The characteristic of Christianity being not to have invented *de nihilo* the three miseries (the three *grandeurs*), death, misery and risk, but to have found their true and proper destination, and to have added sickness, that half of modern man.

And to have assigned to all four their true grandeur, to have given them their full stature.

The religion of antiquity should not be regarded merely as false; it was a surface, a covering, *la religion de dessus*; it was not really of their world, and there was a hiatus between their world and their religion, between the pagan soul and pagan religion. But with Christianity the situation is reversed:

Jesus belongs to the same world as the last of sinners; and the last of sinners belongs to the same world as Jesus. *C'est une communion.* That is really speaking what communion means. And to speak truly or rather to speak *really*, there is no other communion than to belong to the same world.

The pagan soul, as Péguy here uses the expression, is the complete man, more complete than the gods he conceived who were at the best the reflection of his *grandeur* which is hollow without his *misère. Voilà ce que manquent les dieux. Ils manquent de manquer.*

They not only do not know death, they cannot take a risk. Whereas the pagan soul is ripe for the *système de courage*. 'Il était plein, il était nourri de l'âme la plus pieuse, la plus pure, il faut dire le mot, la plus sacrée.' In the modern world that sense of the sacred, the sense of mystery, had been lost.

Péguy's criticism of the modern world is often regarded as the path by which he reached the Christian path. But the theme of the *Commentary* is that it is the intellectuals and the intuitionists who are more concerned to deny than to produce, while Péguy's path, the path which led him on to the Christian path is one of affirmations, the affirmation of freedom as the condition which follows when intellect, will and feeling are united. It is the complete man, the pagan soul which is free, and in that freedom open to grace.

VIII

THE NEW LANGUAGE: IMAGINATION

At the beginning of the *Commentary*, and from the security of his anonymity, Péguy salutes *Eve* and himself as a classic. Not, he goes on to say, a classic of the second generation, the generation of Racine, but a classic of the first generation—placing himself in the company of Corneille, Molière and Pascal. He has often been laughed at for his claim, but if his meaning rather than his claim is examined, the distinction between the first and the second generation ceases to be primarily one of rank (though Péguy certainly meant rank), and becomes an instructive comment on his poetry and his poetic aim.

What Péguy is saying is that the poetic tradition to which he belongs is neither the pure classical tradition of Racine nor the tradition of the French Romantics. This is confirmed by his statement, already quoted, that *Eve* is equally opposed to the 'sterilities of order' (classicism) and the fecundities of disorder (romanticism). Once again he is claiming to be at the centre of tradition.

Péguy's use of the words classical and romantic are only confusing if his distinction between the two generations of classics is overlooked. In itself, no doubt, the distinction defeats his purpose, since it implies the acceptance of two different conceptions of poetry. Péguy was driven to make his unsatisfactory distinction because the French tradition of criticism was too strong for him. Pascal, whom Péguy regards as a classic of the first generation, is as often as not classed as a romantic by those who find that form of classification profitable. Péguy's difficulty, in fact, was due to the failure of the French Romantic movement to evolve a theory of poetry which rose above the stale antithesis between romantic and classic. Sainte-Beuve, who translated the *Aeolian Harp*, would have been better employed making sense of the *Biographia Literaria*. But by the date it appeared, he had soured and turned away from the romantic movement and was content to see nothing in it but romanticism.

Thus by a strange dispensation of fate Péguy's conception of poetry falls more easily into place in the English poetic tradition, and fell on barren soil in his own country. The ideas which he hurriedly dictated to Lotte over a glass of beer, and which most of his French critics make no attempt to interpret, at once unfold in the context of Coleridge's theory of the imagination, reveal their consistency, and more than that, supply the standpoint from which his whole work becomes accessible.

Coleridge on the imagination is a theme which has been treated repeatedly at least since Bradley, and there can hardly be a book on criticism which does not at some point or other take up Coleridge's seminal idea. But such is the vitality of his theory that no two critics need fear saying the same thing in discussing his meaning. With such diversity among Coleridge's interpreters, I make no apology for outlining his theory once again with special reference to Péguy and with the set purpose of using such light as can be obtained from Coleridge to illuminate Péguy, rather than of giving a complete account of the theory of the *Biographia* itself.

If the origin of Coleridge's theory of the imagination is considered, and the character of the *Biographia* as a whole taken into account, there is nothing surprising in the fact that it should have more than a superficial likeness to the

notion of poetry implied in Péguy's work and suggested
in the *Commentary*. In both cases the ideas in question were
linked to the act of conversion. In Péguy's case this is explicitly and undoubtedly so. The *Biographia* with its ramb-
ling, disjointed sequence does not make the relation between Coleridge's theory and his conversion so plain, and
most critics, far from wishing to emphasise the connexion,
are, if anything, at pains to lift the chapter 'On the Imagination' from its context and separate it from Coleridge's
life and philosophy of life, in order to get on with their
own business. But the *Biographia* is an account of Coleridge's life and opinions, of his conversion from Uni-
tarianism to Christianity and belief in the Trinity, and his
theory of the imagination emerges to replace the notion of
poetic creation which had satisfied him as long as he was a
Deist and a rationalist, that is to say a Unitarian. As a
rationalist Coleridge had accepted the 'law of the association of ideas'—as an adequate analysis of the birth of
images. With his conversion the theory ceased to satisfy
him but he did not scrap it altogether. It was then that he
made the distinction between imagination and fancy. But
with his usual laziness Coleridge contented himself with
offering 'the main results' of his chapter on the imagination and avoided the labour and trouble of developing his
idea by writing instead the ironic 'letter from a friend' who
warns him—rightly enough as events have proved— that
no one wants a metaphysical essay on the imagination, but
a useful critical tool. With that 'judicious' letter to hand he
shortened his chapter and set out a couple of definitions
which even in their truncated form continue to inspire the
most diverse schools and have sufficient vitality to irritate
the rest. I give the well-known passage in full, as it is often
shortened.

'The imagination, then, I consider either as primary or secondary. The primary imagination I hold to be the living power and prime agent of all human perception, and as a repetition in the finite mind of the eternal act of creation in the infinite I AM. The secondary imagination I consider as an echo of the former, co-existing in the conscious will, yet still identical with the primary in the kind of its agency, and differing only in *degree*, and in the mode of its operation. It dissolves, diffuses, dissipates, in order to re-create: or where the process is rendered impossible, yet still at all events it struggles to idealise and to unify. It is essentially vital, even as all objects (*as* objects) are essentially fixed and dead.

'*Fancy,* on the contrary, has no other counters to play with but fixities and definites. The fancy is indeed no other than a mode of memory emancipated from the order of time and space; while it is blended with, and modified by that empirical phenomenon of the will, which we express by the word choice. But equally with the ordinary memory, the fancy must receive all its materials ready made from the law of association (of ideas).'

There are two, if not more, distinctions in the definition, both of which are fundamental to Coleridge's meaning. The imagination with which poet and critic are concerned is an *echo* of the primary imagination; and secondly, imagination and fancy are different powers. But it is the first distinction which is the more important and provides the key to the second. This, I think, has not always been made sufficiently evident, largely owing to the form in which the distinctions are made. But although the chapter on imagination was not written, it is not impossible to reconstruct the line of thought which led to the 'main results'.

The secondary imagination is the creative power which gives form to the vision or perception of the primary imagination, and though different in the mode of its operation, which is active (while the primary imagination is receptive), it is not different in kind. Elsewhere, Coleridge describes its formation and operation in the following terms:

'The poet, described in ideal perfection, brings the whole soul of man into activity, with the subordination of its faculties to each other, according to their relative worth and dignity. He diffuses a tone and a spirit of unity that blends and (as it were) fuses each into each, by that synthetic and magical power to which I should exclusively appropriate the name of Imagination.'

In this passage Coleridge describes in his own way what Péguy describes in the *Commentary* as a descent to the point at which the spiritual life and the spiritual proposition, the idea and the image, are as yet undifferentiated. Both of them are attempting to describe the poetic power as the fruit of the harmony and unity of vision, in which not one faculty alone is active, but the whole soul of man. Their conception of imagination is so close to Kierkegaard's that I shall quote his more deliberate definition:

'The imagination,' he writes, 'is not one faculty on a par with others, but, if one may so speak, it is the faculty *instar omnium*, which replaces all the others. What feeling, knowledge or will a man has, depends in the last resort on what imagination he has, that is to say, upon how these things are reflected [or as Coleridge says, echoed] i.e., it depends upon imagination. Imagination is the reflection of the process of infinitising, and hence the elder Fichte [from whom Coleridge no doubt took a hint without mentioning it] quite rightly assumed, even in relation to knowledge,

that imagination is the origin of the categories [and Coleridge, the agent of perception]; it is a counterfeit present-
ment [or echo] of the self, which is the possibility of the
self, and the intensity of this medium corresponds to the
possible intensity of the self.'

Kierkegaard is speaking principally of the 'primary
imagination', as the faculty *instar omnium* which focuses
and fuses all man's faculties, and he goes on to analyse the
forms of despair into which the self disintegrates if 'the
whole soul' is not brought into activity. Then, he writes,
echoing Coleridge's term, the self which does not mature
and come to unity in the imagination becomes *fantastical*,
and either feeling, or knowledge or will so dominates that
man runs headlong into the fantastic and loses touch with
reality. Rationalism, voluntarism or sentimentality is the
result. All three forms of disintegration are forms of
despair, of flight from reality, whereas imagination is the
possibility of maturity (the 'self'), and the possibility of
faith. It is only when all the faculties are co-ordinated that
man begins to exist and as he writes: 'Man only begins to
exist in faith.' But while Kierkegaard is mainly concerned
with the nature of the primary imagination, his preoccu-
pation with the problem of communication shows that
for him communication is an echo of the primary imagination, the faculty of expressing the total vision of man and
the fruit of experience. But the problem only arises for
those who, like Péguy, recognise the equal rights of
'pathos' and reason (or, as Kierkegaard says, of pathos and
dialectics) when the *form* of communication itself becomes
significant and is inseparable from the content which it
qualifies decisively. That is why all three, Coleridge,
Kierkegaard and Péguy, arrived at a parallel conception of
imagination and communication at the turning point in

their lives, their conversion. The same is true, as has already been noted, of Pascal.

There is one further point with regard to the imagination which calls for clarification before returning to Péguy's poetry. In his lectures on *The Poetic Image*, Mr. Day Lewis raises a question on which the majority of critics find themselves at variance with the romantic view of imagination. He quotes Sidney who tells us how the poet 'yieldeth to the power of the mind an image of that whereof the philosopher bestoweth but a worthless description, which doth neither strike, pierce nor possess the sight of the soul, so much as that other doth'. And there is Ben Jonson for whom poetry is 'a dulcet and gentle philosophy, which leads on and guides us by the hand to action.' But apart from didactic poetry 'where in any case the metaphorical level is usually shallow' Mr. Day Lewis finds it difficult to conceive that verse can make us act. He is not disposed to accept Charles Williams's view that certain lines can 'awaken in us a sense that we are capable of love and sacrifice'. Poetry, he feels, should not have an object beyond itself, or, as Kierkegaard says, it is not written 'in order that . . .'

But what Shelley says, more accurately than Sidney or Jonson or Charles Williams, is that 'the great instrument of moral good' is the imagination. And if Coleridge's distinction is preserved, it is clear what the writers of this school are driving at. It is not poetry *as such* which guides us by the hand to action, but the primary imagination which may of course be echoed in the creation of the secondary imagination, poetry. For one of the characteristics of the imagination is that it does lead to action, whereas reason or sentiment alone and isolated do not. 'Images when assented to,' Newman writes, 'have an influence on individuals and society, which mere notions cannot exert' and the argument of the *Grammar of Assent* is yet another attempt to depict the co-ordination of notional and real assent (real assent to images) and their fusion in the illative sense which is a parallel to imagination in the sense of Coleridge.* For belief which is primarily notional, a faith which is assent to certain propositions is colourless, whereas when faith is informed by what Newman calls real assent, which involves the imagination, it is 'as living as the imagination itself', and this means to say that it not only leads on to action, but is enriched and deepened by action. And this, it will be seen, is an essential facet of Péguy's conception of faith, and the definition of his *mystique*.

The imagination, then, is 'essentially *vital*' and its operation is to re-create, or, if that is not possible, to idealise and unify what it sees. Its sight or vision is not preternatural or strange, but the vision of the complete man. But the modern poet, according to Coleridge, 'sacrifices the passion and the passionate flow of poetry (the unity of vision) to the glare and glitter of a perpetual, yet broken and heterogeneous imagery, or rather an amphibious something made up half of image, half of abstract meaning'— he does not remain at the point at which idea and image, abstract and concrete, are as yet one.

But the 'passionate flow of poetry,' the sustained unity

---

* *The Grammar of Assent* is Newman's mature development of the ideas first outlined in the *University Sermons*. 'The author,' he there says in a footnote, 'was not acquainted at the time this was written with Mr. Coleridge's works, and a remarkable passage in his *Biographia Literaria* in which several portions of this Sermon are anticipated. It has been pointed out to him since by the kindness of a friend. *Vide Biog. Lit.* Vol I, p. 199.' Both Newman and Coleridge would profit from being read in conjunction.

of vision requires that the theme so passionately envisaged should at the same time be 'remote from private interests'. This is the point at which Péguy is farthest from contemporary poetry. He is equidistant from the Augustan poet whose theme is not passionately conceived, and from the intensity expressed in the glitter of heterogenous imagery. Like Wordsworth he is 'not always graceful . . . in the play of fancy' and unlike Wordsworth he could neither prune nor improve his epic after he had written it. The *ton* or 'climate' seemed everything to him, the sustained unity of imaginative vision. His poetry has to get along as best it can without the help of fancy, and the technical skill which goes with it, which is to say that it often falls flat or into interminable *longueurs*. Péguy has no resources at such times, and can only wait till he is lifted up again by his imagination. These uninspired passages leave him with a theme remote from private interests, which becomes lifeless the moment it is not passionately conceived.

The theme of all, or at any rate of most of Péguy's poetry is Christian faith, the life of grace. He is not writing about his own belief, his faith in certain propositions, but of the new life and vision. What he contemplates in prayer he communicates in his poetry.

'What others know,' Madame Gervaise says to Joan, 'you *see*. All we are taught, you *see*. The Catechism, the Church, the Mass, you don't just know them, you *see* them; prayer, you don't say your prayers, you didn't only say them, you *see* them.'

In that sense Péguy's poetry is his prayer. But the theme is not, as this might suggest, a private matter. Faith itself is not a private matter. Faith, hope and charity in these poems are not private but the opposite, personal: for what is most personal is turned away from the private sphere and to be personal means to be related to others. Grace is the freedom to relinquish the private sphere of egoism and enter the field of communion. Faith, to Péguy, is characterised by communion; poetry is communication. But faith is also the light in which he sees, not his light, but the light given in grace, and it is specially in this sense that he speaks of himself as *gracié*, graced. He is not interested in his 'experience' but in what he sees and his poetry is the immediate, direct communication, as simple as possible, of what he saw. He could put his major poems into the mouth of God as though to illustrate Coleridge's theory that the imagination is a repetition in the finite mind of the infinite act of creation in the infinite I AM.

But it would, I think, be confusing to call Péguy a mystical poet if by that is meant a poet for whom meadow, grove and stream are so many intimations of immortality. They are, it is true, apparelled for him in celestial light, but it is the light which comes first which gives them their significance. 'The things which I have seen I now can see no more' is not the whole truth. Faith is not the recollection of childhood, but its renewal, the renewal of innocence which is the theme of *The Holy Innocents*. For Péguy's *mystique* is not mysticism, but faith 'as living as the imagination' and consequently incommunicable except through the imagination. He is not an evocative poet, but the poet of invocation. And just as he regarded *la mystique* as the source of all vital *politiques*, so it was the source of his poetry.

Tout le jaillissement dans le germe, tout l'ordre dans l'épi is the primal law of Péguy's thought. All the vitality and freedom is in the germ, and creates the order in life and the form of the poem. The form is in no sense a limitation of freedom but its expression. And the more powerful the imagination the more imposing the form. Tradition is the handing down of the freedom to create new forms, the capacity as Burckhardt says for renaissances which can only come to full fruition where the spirit is released through the harmony of all the faculties, when the whole soul of man is brought into activity.

IX

THE *CAHIERS* 1908–1914

Péguy's conversion was not the end of his life and work but the beginning. All that he had written down to the summer of 1907 is the prelude to his mature work. This is no less true of the prose *Notre Jeunesse, Victor-Marie, Comte Hugo,* the two versions of *Clio,* and the *Note Conjointe,* than of the poetry, which emerged and clarified his whole outlook. Péguy himself was overwhelmed by the revelation of his new powers. The freedom which he loved above everything was no longer an idea or an ideal but a virtue, a power, the power to create, and for a moment it seemed to him as though his whole life was to change.

For roughly two years after the appearance of *De la situation faite à l'Histoire dans le monde moderne,* published in the summer of 1907, he wrote nothing. His only contribution to the new series of *Cahiers* was an appeal to his readers to redouble their support: *à nos amis à nos abonnés,* 1909. He was undecided whether what he now had to say could be said through the medium of the *Cahiers,* and he began to believe that as a Catholic he would no longer have to struggle in isolation. He had fought for so long against crippling odds that as he entered the new phase of his life, sustained by a new-found hope, optimism got the better of him. He was no longer unknown and he began to think that success was round the corner; and as he settled down to *Notre Jeunesse* and the *Mystères,* he had no doubt about it. Barrès, in 1910, advised him not to bother with the Académie des Goncourts: 'Ça masque l'Académie. Je réponds, c'est très joli, l'Académie Française, mais je ne l'aurais pas avant dix ou quinze ans, et d'ici là il faut que j'élève mes enfants.' But Barrès put the Academy at three or four years. 'So you see, old man,' he said to Lotte, '*j'aurais la gloire avant l'argent* . . . Living is still as difficult as it was ten years ago. But it doesn't matter. All of a sudden things will begin to move.'

Péguy was thinking as though he were a convert, the sort of convert the Catholics wanted and liked, another Bourget or Brunetière, putting his pen at their disposal. He reckoned on their understanding and left his temperament out of account. The lesson of the Librairie Georges Bellais was forgotten in the excitement, and he no longer remembered how soon the Socialist leaders found they could do without his help and how quickly they scented an anarchist in their midst. Péguy was given a second lesson. The quarrels began almost at once, and he soon discovered that his original estimate of the Catholic party had been correct. The last thing they wanted was anything new.

'Paris, Friday 1st April 1910. From now on, old man, my whole production can be realised within the framework of *Jeanne d'Arc*. [The first *Mystère* was published in January of that year.] I foresee a dozen volumes. I can put everything into it. Just think, the war, the King, politics, the Sorbonne. Oh, the Doctors ! . . . the same as ever . . . . *les bougres n'ont pas changé. Jeanne d'Arc* offered a form of sanctity which was not labelled, catalogued; not a note that fits her case; so it was perfectly clear, she was a demoniac! Oh, the cretins ! They're all the same, the intellectuals.'*

---

*This letter and the remaining quotations in this section are from the *Lettres et Entretiens* of Péguy and Lotte which were collected by Quoniam mentioned before. They have recently been republished by Marcel Péguy.

But the *Mystery of the Charity of Joan of Arc* did not make
the impression which he hoped for. His first public profession of faith fell flat. Not even Tharaud understood him,
and the Catholics were more than hesitant to recognise
him. In his attempt to make Péguy better known to the
Catholic public, his confidant, Joseph Lotte, met with
some astonishing reverses.

'Only, if I am to publish your article,' wrote one editor,
'you must give me permission to disavow any responsibility from the doctrinal point of view as far as my review
is concerned . . . I must admit that I do not at all share
your admiration for some of the sentiments in the drama,
in particular as regards the soul of Mary, even allowing
that she is seen through the eyes and soul of an old peasant,
or rather a cook; *ah, non,* that doesn't seem to me at all the
thing, it is the act of a man whom one would barely sup-
pose Christian . . . It all seems to me to be the work of a
gentleman rather poorly informed about our Christianity . . .'

Péguy's discouragement was, however, soothed for the
moment by the success of *Notre Jeunesse*, even though it
involved him in some difficulties with Halévy, to whom it
was a reply. Barrès, Tharaud, and most of the friends who
had supported him in the past, were full of praise for the
account of Péguy's long duel in the Dreyfus Affair. But as
soon as he began to express his Catholicism they no longer
followed him, and the new audience he hoped to reach
rejected his advances.

Victor-Marie, Comte Hugo, a continuation of some of the
themes of *Notre Jeunesse*, again raised his hopes. Barrès and
a number of others supported him for the Academy prize,
and he was within an inch of being chosen. Romain
Rolland's candidature was fatal to his chances, and his

failure, he realised, wrecked his chances of being elected to the Academy. Lotte, who noted their talks, was, however, instructed to push for his election. 'Financially the situation is still very strained, but one must not let up and do everything possible to increase subscriptions. Speak of me as of a *maître*: say negligently in the course of conversation, Péguy will soon be in the Academy. *Ça fait très bien . . .*

'*Acker m'est très utile. Il connait un tas de femmes. C'est épatant, un type comme cela. Il couche avec les vieilles, et c'est moi qui vais en profiter. Enorme!*'

But in spite of his naïve attempts at intrigue, he was beginning to realise the difficulty of his situation. Bourgeois, Péguy's faithful assistant at the office of the *Cahiers*, was alarmed at the future prospects 'à cause de la bassesse intellectuelle et morale du parti clérical qui règne dans l'Eglise'.

In his candidature for the Academy Péguy was supported by the extreme Right and put down his failure to the influence of the Left and the 'intellectuals' he had always attacked. Among the Catholics, it was the extreme Right that were most suspicious, and he was sharply taken to task in an article in the *Revue Hebdomadaire* which he answered in a new *Cahier: Un nouveau théologien, M. Fernand Laudet*. Lotte was the first to feel the draught, when two Bishops wrote and asked not to receive his Bulletin, in which Péguy had defended himself. Politically speaking he was still where he had always been, at the centre, at war with both extremes, with the Clericals and anti-Clericals.

Péguy's position was much more delicate than ever before, for now his private life was beset with difficulties. He had married outside the Church, and none of his children were baptised. The story has been told countless times, not always with tact, and can be reduced to the fact that Péguy refused to dissociate himself in any way from his wife, who could not agree to a religious ceremony. He remained, in consequence, technically outside the Church. It was then, during the period of his greatest trials, that his son Pierre fell dangerously ill with diphtheria, and Péguy made his pilgrimage to Chartres, dedicating his children to Our Lady of Chartres.

The pilgrimage marks a turning point in Péguy's life at this time, and it seems as though he himself dated a new period from the 23rd August, 1912:

'I left my heart there and I think I shall be buried there. I received extraordinarary graces there; and it is the only place where I could perhaps go beyond a certain point in confession.'

But he felt that a barrier had been placed between him and the Catholics, a barrier which was in fact political in origin, as he was to explain in the *Note Conjointe*. It was after that pilgrimage, the second according to the chronology worked out by Marcel Péguy, that he wrote to Lotte, that he had no plans: *il ne faut pas suivre de plan, il faut suivre des indications.*

'I have changed a lot in the last two years. I am a new man. I have suffered so much and prayed so much. If you lived nearby, you would know everything. But when one only meets twice a year! I can't explain it all to you. I live without the sacraments. It's a risk. But I have treasures of grace, an inconceivable, super-abundance of grace. I follow the indications. One must never resist. Little Pierre fell ill with diphtheria, in August, as he arrived at the sea-side. Then, old man, I felt things were serious. I had to make a vow—above all, don't mention it in your Bulletin—I made a pilgrimage to Chartres. I come from the Beauce. Chartres is my Cathedral. I was not all worked up. I did a hundred and forty-four kilometres in three days . . . One can see the spire of Chartres seventeen kilometres away on the plain. From time to time it disappears behind an undulation, a line of wood. From the moment I saw it, it was ecstasy. All my impurities fell from me at once. I was a different man. I prayed for an hour in the Cathedral on Sunday morning, before High Mass. I did not assist at Mass. I was afraid of the crowds. I prayed, old man, as I have never prayed. I prayed for my enemies; which had never happened to me. And when I say my enemies, I don't mean Laudet, as you can imagine; I can pray for that sort every day. But there are certain kinds of enemies, certain enemies, and if I had to pray for them in normal times, I should infallibly have a liver attack; no, my liver simply wouldn't let me. My boy is saved, I gave them all three to Our Lady. I can't look after everything. My life is not an ordinary one. My life is a stake. No one is a prophet in his own country. My children are not baptised, so it's up to the Blessed Virgin to look after them. I have an office, enormous responsibilities. At bottom it's a Catholic renaissance which is happening through me. One must see things as they are and hold on.

'I am a sinner, not a saint. Sanctity can be recognised at once. I am a sinner, a good sinner. The finest prayer to Our Lady was written by Villon. I am a Chronicler, a witness, a Christian in the parish, a sinner, but a sinner who has treasures of grace, and an astonishing Guardian Angel. More than once, old man, I have taken decisions. It couldn't last. I had resolved to abdicate in everything. I accepted the ill towards which I was going, and my Guardian Angel simply set it aside. I was remade. Oh, the moralists, the protestants, the jansenists . . . they understand nothing. There is nothing so un-Christian as moralism . . .

'So I abandon myself. I no longer hold to anything. *La gloire* which interested me two years ago, *je m'en fous*. I abandon myself. I follow the counsel that God gives in *The Holy Innocents*. The *Innocents* was an anticipation. I had never practised what I expressed there. Now I abandon myself.

'Ultimately there are two kinds of sin, two sorts of creatures. There are creatures who are given grace, *graciées*. Grace comes to them, it's an astonishing mystery. There are creatures who are not graced. Why? No one knows. It has nothing to do with salvation. Salvation is another matter. The saints draw all they can into heaven, graced and ungraced. But what one must realise is that the geography, the map of Catholicism, of the Church, does not coincide with the map of those who are graced . . .

'One must not see everything in black. Our race has inexhaustible resources. The coming generation is splendid. When one hears idiots like Léon Bloy proclaiming that Paris is going to crumble under a hail of fire as a punishment for its crimes, one can only shrug one's shoulders.'

A year later he was sure of his position, he no longer thought of the Academy or money. Hence *L'argent* and *L'argent suite*.

'My situation is tremendous, corresponding exactly to my misery. It's settled; it's a life sentence. I do not expect any change. When Quoniam (who collected his MSS.) becomes a millionaire, perhaps we'll have a good time. In the meantime everything is all right as it is: unbelievable trials in the private sphere, immense graces for my production. I am the only one who can say certain things, so I say them. You cannot imagine the abundance of grace. I see quite simple things. It amazes the priests: the liturgy is full of them; they have never seen them. So they are suspicious. When I am dead they will begin to have confidence . . . One must produce. One must not prove, demonstrate or explain. Pascal reasons too much, so the unbelievers get the ropes on him *et se foutent de lui* . . . But I create. One must create. Listen, I shall cover the same surface in a Christian sense as Goethe did in a pagan.'

Péguy was fully launched in the second, poetic, phase of his work: *The Mystery of the Charity of Joan of Arc* was followed by two more *Mystères*, by the *Sonnets,* the *Quatrains,* the *Tapestries,* and by the epic in which he summed up all he had to say. In all, fourteen hundred pages in the Pléiade edition: a poetic work as central and eccentric as the prose out of which it sprang.

X

THE *MYSTERIES*

When Péguy left the Church as a young man and looked for salvation in the Socialist movement he began by writing *Jeanne d'Arc*. In the 1898 version he had left a large number of blank pages which, he informed his friends, was to give them time to think. On his return to the Church he took up his *oeuvre de jeunesse* and intended to re-write the whole work, filling in the blanks. In fact he only recast the first scene or so and then went on to the *Porche* and *The Holy Innocents*.

Joan is Péguy's patron. It is Joan who gives his life and work their unity. If he left the Church, it was in her company, and because he continued to believe in her he returned. She is the real influence in his life, the inspiration of his *fidélité*, the centre of the 'invisible parish', the invisible Church which moved 'secretly within him'. All the external influences which played about him in those early years, Sorel and Bergson and Michelet, the influence of his friends, of his opponents, are extraneous by comparison with the mysterious link which he contracted as a young man, the strength of which he could not realise till it had borne fruit. He learnt technically from others, but as Kierkegaard says, the autodidact in the spiritual sphere is a theodidact; Joan was his patron saint in the true sense, who led him to God. And just as his poetry can be seen emerging from his prose in certain pages of the *Mystery*, his faith can be seen struggling to the light, from hesitation to hope and from hope to joy in the final version of *Jeanne d'Arc* and its two sequels.

Through Joan's life Péguy came to understand his own life; in her mission he discovered the relation between *la mystique* and *la politique*, and in her faith the relation between *le salut temporel* and *le salut éternel*.

The first *Joan* is dedicated 'to all those who give their lives to remedy the universal evil, and for the establishment of the universal Socialist republic'. The dedication should have been enough to correct Rolland's impression that Péguy had no desire to unify the world, but having failed to understand what Péguy meant by unity he overlooked the frantic optimism of the dedication and only saw the pessimism of the text. For in the first *Joan* Péguy was still torn between optimism and pessimism, conscious of *le mal universal* and the penury of the modern world on the one hand, and righting his balance by catching at the optimistic theories of Socialism and progress. The dedication instances his optimism. In the text he unloads all his pessimism on to Joan. His faith is hardly more than his belief in her faith, the faith in the faith of others which betokened freedom. He did not believe when he wrote the first *Joan*; he only believed in her faith. That was the first step in his system of courage. Her courage gave him courage.

I know your suffering (he makes Madame Gervaise say to Joan), I know the suffering that seems so terrible to you, and beyond endurance; you have seen that all those whom you love are cowardly; you have seen that your father is cowardly and that your mother is cowardly.

It is tempting to trace back all Péguy's thought to that beginning because it illustrates as nothing else can do the consistency of his thought and explains why he was to call it years afterwards 'a system of courage', not in any metaphorical sense but without affectation, and without exaggeration. Moreover, anyone who reads the early scenes of the first *Joan* will probably be more tempted to wonder whether Péguy ever gave up his faith, rather than to regard the *Mystery* as the token of his return. But in the first version Madame Gervaise has no answer, or only a formal, official answer to Joan's despair at the cowardice of those around her—just as Péguy could not fully answer the weakness and cowardice of those who refused to stand alone and took refuge in the artificial unity of the two parties which stood face to face. He perceived their cowardice clearly enough, he saw the weakness of their politics, and their lack of spirituality, of faith in their own beliefs and their refusal to believe in the faith of others, but at first he was only supported by his Socialism, the one cure for *le mal universel.*

This ambiguity has suggested to most critics that Joan's despair represents Péguy's point of view and Madame Gervaise's confidence that of the Church. There may be an element of truth in the interpretation, but to use it as a key to Péguy's thought whether in 1898 or in 1908 is to obscure his consistency and the change which came about during the years that followed; a change which is not in contradiction with the beginning but is its fulfilment.

In the first *Joan* Madame Gervaise reproves Joan for her despair over the loss and damnation of souls and the destruction of Christendom which Péguy was subsequently to see as the de-christianisation of France in his own day. But Madame Gervaise has no remedy; or rather the remedy stands in no sort of proportion to the evil. Her answer to Joan is that 'Jesus preached; Jesus prayed; Jesus

suffered. We must imitate him with all our might.' Her
answer is a parallel to Péguy's later account of this period
during which, he says, he observed 'the deepest lessons of
the Gospels'. But the devil of his despair was not to be
driven out by prayer and fasting alone. In the second version Joan is still overwhelmed by despair as she contemplates the state of Christendom, the failure as it seems to her
of Christianity, the vanity of charity, the failure of the Incarnation itself. She contrasts the parishes of Christendom
in her own day (in Péguy's day), deserted, destitute and
desecrated, with the first days of Christendom when
Christ was on earth surrounded by his disciples—though
he does not forget St. Peter's denial, his lack of faith and
cowardice. It is as though the eternal had come into time
but not to remain there; and if there were no eternal salvation, how could there be a temporal salvation?

Joan's despairing monologue is magnificently expanded
in the second version and Madame Gervaise's entry is de-
layed; and when she appears it is not to reprove and
answer Joan but to join with her in singing the praise of
the mystery of the faith which brings hope with it. Without greeting one another, the two women intone their
invocation together, *en vision à elles deux*:

> He is there.
> He is there as on the first day.
> He is there, among us, as on the day of his death.
> Eternally there, among us, as on the first day.
>
> His body, his very body, hangs on the same cross;
> His eyes, the same eyes, tremble with the same tears;
>
> The same blood flows in the self-same sacrifice.
> The same thing which happened in those times
>   happens every day, on every day of eternity.

In all the parishes of Christendom.
Israel, Israel, you do not know how great you are;
But you too, Christians, do not know your greatness;
Your present greatness; which is the same greatness;
Your eternal greatness.

From this point on the dialogue is tautened, the style smoulders and by the end of the scene Péguy's *vers libre* is born.

The eternal has entered into time; *l'insertion de l'éternel dans le temporel* is not a past event, the token of man's eternal salvation, but through the Church and the sacraments, through the Eucharist, is the ever-present source of his salvation, both eternal and temporal. And, as though to emphasise once again the mystery of faith, the first of the poems ends with a question. 'What do we know?' Madame Gervaise asks. 'We are in the hands of God. The ways of God are unfathomable.'

The certainty of faith, Péguy seems to say, is not seen in faith itself, but in hope, the theme of the next two *Mysteries*. For faith remains a system of courage, and its courage and freedom are expressed in hope. In a sense Péguy had always believed. But his faith was only complete when he saw it joined to hope as well as charity. No other writer has given such prominence to hope, bringing what is so often a distant and abstract 'supernatural virtue' to life. Hope, to Péguy, is the most mysterious of the theological virtues, whose natural counterpart is freedom, the virtue that prevents faith from hardening into a sterile tradition and leaves it open to the future, capable of growth and freedom.

The three mysteries form a triptych. In the second, *Le Porche du Mystère de la Deuxième Vertu,* Péguy expresses his

hope, though it is not until the third panel that he enters
'the unknown domain, the strange domain of joy. A hundred times less known, a hundred times more strange, than
the kingdom of sorrow.'

Le Porche opens with a hymn to hope spoken by
Madame Gervaise, but put into the mouth of God the
Father.

> The faith I like best, God says, is hope.
> Faith does not astonish me.
> It's not astonishing.
> I literally explode in my creation.
> In the sun and the moon and in the stars.
>
> Charity, God says, does not astonish me.
> It's not astonishing.
>
> But hope, God says, does astonish me.
>   I myself.
> That is astonishing.
>
> Faith sees what is.
> In time and in eternity.
> Hope sees what will be.
> In time and in eternity.
>
> In the future of eternity itself, so to say.

The *Mystery of the Holy Innocents* begins in almost the
same words as the *Porche* and is another set of variations
on the same theme: hope. Faith, he begins, looks as though
it were everything, and hope looks as though it were
almost nothing. Faith is the oak tree, and hope is only the
bud on the branch. But the bud is the sign of life, the
promise of the future breaking out of the past, *le nouveau
réel* and *le jaillissement*. 'La rude écorce n'est rien, que du
bois durci, que du bourgeon vieilli. Et c'est pour cela que

le tendre bourgeon perce toujours, jaillit toujours dessous la dure écorce.'

It is hope that keeps faith young, and through hope it becomes the source of the 'eternal renaissance' which is the mark of a living faith and a live tradition. And but for that bud, which a child can break off, everything would be dead: 'toute ma création ne serait que du bois mort. Et le bois mort sera jeté au feu.'

C'est le tronc et la branche, et cette maîtresse racine qui sont faits pour la résistance, qui sont chargés de résister . . .

Mais le tendre bourgeon n'est fait que pour la naissance et il n'est chargé que de faire naître.

The three *Mysteries* give, as it were, the sequence of Péguy's return to Catholicism, the sequence of the coming of grace. In a sense he had always believed, but he had not always hoped, and it was hope that transfigured his natural fidelity into supernatural faith that brought his faith fully alive. For the mission of hope is 'to bring to birth'.

The *Mysteries* are not 'mystery plays', though Péguy had them in mind when he chose the title. They are *Mysteries* because they are variations on a single theme, the mysteries of the faith, hope and charity, the life of grace. It is in these three poems that Péguy communicates to others the concrete and personal faith, hope and charity, the spiritual seed which, because it is free, creates the unity of Catholicism. Moreover, communication now assumes its full form and meaning and ends in communion.

The Christian is not defined by his level but by communion. One is not a Christian because one is at a certain moral, intellectual or even spiritual level. One is a Christian because one belongs to a certain race that goes back in time, a certain mystical race, a spiritual and carnal race, temporal and spiritual alike, because one is of a certain blood.

Commenting on this passage, André Rousseaux observes that it is the blood of Christ that engenders the new race and remedies the universal evil that had held Péguy in despair. That is another reason why Péguy avoids the word conversion with its suggestion of a private event. The essence of the mystery of faith, hope and charity is that it is a form of communion and not an intellectual or moral or even spiritual conversion. *Les Catholiques*, he said to Lotte in 1912, *sont vraiment insupportables dans leur sécurité mystique. Le propre de la mystique est au contraire une inquiétude invincible.* Hope, because it is *chargé de faire naître*, is the guarantor that the certainty of faith is not allowed to degenerate into desire for security but remains open to the future, 'charged to bring [the future] to birth'. The life of faith, hope and charity in Péguy's work is expressed in the mission which it imposes. Separated from that mission, allowed to avoid the problem of communication, it ceases to be a communion and comes to be judged by the moral, intellectual and spiritual level. Then *la mystique* alters in character, is referred to a private world, and becomes falsely divorced from *la politique* or submerged in a particular *politique*.

XI

LA MYSTIQUE ET LA POLITIQUE IN THE MODERN WORLD

Péguy's use of the words *mystique* and *politique* has suffered the usual fate attached to the word mysticism. The confusion of thought which the word sets in motion has been almost impossible to halt. Bainville, for example, the historian of the *Action Française*, refers patronisingly to Péguy's 'primitive mystique' which in a writer who is not otherwise obtuse in his special pleading, suggest a touch of *ressentiment*. His irritation would not be worth recalling but for the fact that it illustrates so well the intellectual atmosphere in Péguy's day. Bainville, like Maurras, had no time for mysticism which they equated with romanticism, except possibly with the proviso that it was rigidly controlled, rendered harmless and preferably segregated.

The best-known passages on *la mystique* and *la politique* occur in *Notre Jeunesse,* but any ambiguity which might be attributed to his use of the words has been finally dispelled by the publication of the first version of *Clio*.* From internal evidence it must have been written at the same time, subsequently discarded in favour of the second version (published posthumously) and left with four or five other half-finished works. It is in that very important unfinished *Cahier* that Péguy explains what he means by *mystique,* not in the confusing context of *la politique,* as he does in *Notre Jeunesse,* but as the Christian mission, or

*Under the title *Deuxième Elégie XXX*, Gallimard, 1955.

what he calls 'the Christian operation'. In a selection of Péguy's work it would follow immediately on the *Mysteries* so that the faith, hope and charity of the three poems could be seen as 'the Christian operation', and eternal salvation not segregated from the temporal salvation of man.

Originally (he there says), primitively, the mystical life, the Christian operation consisted not in avoiding the world, but in saving the world, not in fleeing from the times (*le siècle*), in separating and cutting oneself off and hiding away from the times, but *on the contrary*, it consisted in nourishing the times mystically.

The mystical life, that is to say, the supernatural life of faith, hope and charity, which is the theme of the *Mysteries,* is seen here as 'the Christian operation', the mission of Christianity in the world. Péguy's contemplation of faith and hope leads directly into action and the fulcrum preserving the balance between the two is charity.

Far from silencing his criticism of Catholicism as it functioned in the nineteenth century and in his own day, Péguy's return to the Church sharpened his awareness of its shortcomings. In the earlier *Cahiers* his criticism amounted to little more than applying the moral standard which he applied to the Socialists with equal impartiality to the Catholics. After the *Mysteries* the test is no longer the moral one, but a more severe standard, the Christian mission: Christendom itself. The attack on the Catholicism of his day in the first *Clio* is the immediate result of his rediscovery of the Catholic tradition, for if the mission of Christianity in its Catholic form was to be carried out, the first requirement was a clear view of the times, of the *monde moderne*, and an analysis of the failure of

Christianity—which in the first *Joan* had seemed to him irremediable.

Since Péguy's death, a good deal of his criticism of nineteenth-century Catholicism has become current coin and is in danger of becoming an end in itself. Moreover, it is not his particular criticisms which are of permanent value. They were concerned with a particular time and place. His 'true value' is to be found in the point of view from which they are made.

At first sight it might almost be thought that Péguy was thinking in terms of the regeneration of society and the reconciliation of Catholicism and the modern world.

Christianity in the modern world is no longer what it was—of the people . . . Christianity is no longer socially the religion of the depths . . . Socially it is nothing more than the religion of the bourgeois, the religion of the rich, a wretched sort of distinguished religion . . . Everything, in fact, that is most contrary to its institution, to holiness, to poverty—to the Gospels. The Church in fact is the formal religion of the rich. It is therefore nothing; that is why it means nothing. (*Notre Jeunesse.*)

That had been Péguy's view from the first, and in one of the earliest *Cahiers* he had made the same point.

We must not withdraw from the living world, in order to contemplate a celestial city. It seems to me that humanity at the present time needs the whole care of all men. No doubt it would have less need for our work if the religious men who preceded us had worked a little more humanly, or if they had prayed less. For to pray is not to work.

But as Roman Rolland says, Péguy certainly no longer maintained that prayer was not work. After 1908 the source of all his 'work' was his prayer, so that he could hardly distinguish between inspiration, genius and grace. His prayer, his contemplation flowed into action and this he translated by saying that *la mystique* must be the source of *la politique*. And in the *Mystery of the Charity of Joan of Arc* he makes Joan say: 'Prier, se battre. Ni l'un sans l'autre. Ni l'autre sans l'un. Mais l'un et l'autre ensemble, tous les deux.' Almost everything in his life can be traced back to Joan, but most clearly of all his conception of his mission and of the relation between *la mystique* and *la politique*, of a living Christendom which he calls in *Notre Jeunesse* 'a religion of temporal salvation which would give health to the *monde ouvrier*, giving dignity to work, restoring the industrial world, in the mud of which Christianity itself has got bogged, Christianity which is the religion of eternal salvation'.

Péguy's criticism of *le monde moderne* bulks so large in his work that it sometimes conceals his real purpose: to understand 'the Christian operation' not in the abstract, but in the concrete situation in which he found himself. Considered in isolation it has even been read to mean that he abandoned Socialism and watered it down into a prudent, conservative plea for a little more social justice, or as though he was making the gambit of the Catholic Right complaining morosely of the evil of modern times. From this it is only a step to identifying his phrases about the parish of the fifteenth century and his notion of Christendom with a nostalgic longing for the Christendom of the Middle Ages, that legacy of a false romanticism. There are many links between Péguy's work and the romantic movement, but that is not one of them.

Péguy's attitude to the modern world is altogether more complex; it varied, changed and may even appear to be self-contradictory; but it was never simply one of rejection. There are of course times in the *Cahiers*, and particularly in *Eve*, when he gives the impression that the modern world is altogether corrupt and unredeemable. Most of the time Péguy is talking simultaneously on two levels, writing on two staves. There is the *monde moderne* in the strictly limited sense, which he treated as beginning about 1881; there is the *monde moderne* inaugurated by the Revolution; but there is also the *monde moderne*, the contemporary world which Christendom always has before it, which is not the same as 'the world' in the scriptural sense, however opposed it may be at one time or another to Christianity. All these worlds are 'the world' which it is the mission of Christianity to nourish mystically so that it should not become the prey of politics and power. These distinctions emerge gradually and become significant as Péguy's Catholicism becomes explicit. And though the tirade against the modern world in *Eve* is more unbridled than any which precedes it, his violence is balanced by his greater hope, and by his growing sense that alongside its corruption lies a great achievement only waiting to be nourished by the Christian *mystique*. What had begun as an attack ended in a discriminating attitude to the modern world.

Péguy's earliest essay on the history of the modern world was not published during his lifetime. It forms the greater part of *Par ce demi-clair Matin* written in 1906. There is only one moment in history, he says there, one movement in history, which he rejects utterly: the 'stupid and odious political and social reactions of the Restoration' in France. The *monde moderne* was 'inaugurated' by the Revolution, but it had been built through the ages, by Louis IX and Louis XI, by Richelieu and Louis XIV. The

Revolution 'inaugurated' the modern world, but that did not, in Péguy's eyes, involve a break with the past. The real breach, the real break in tradition came with the Restoration when, for the first time, the monarchy broke with its own past. It was the Counter-Revolution and not the Revolution that involved the final separation of tradition and freedom. (He regards Louis XVI as a double figure, half of whose reign, half of whose work, was in conformity with the history of the monarchy, the other half of whose work sowed the seeds of reaction.) One of his main criticisms of the contemporary world is its blindness to the legacy of the monarchy, its failure to distinguish between the monarchy which prepared the way for Revolution, and the monarchy which tried to undo the work of the Revolution. That is why he spoke of *La République notre Royaume de France*, to the annoyance of both parties.

The *monde moderne* in its limited sense, which he dates from about 1881 (roughly with the rise of Boulangisme and, as he maintains, with the collapse of the Republican *mystique*), is painted at first in the darkest of colours as a world marked by 'a horrible indigence, a horrible penury of the sacred'—the world in which there is no soul and no community, no piety and no mystery, fundamentally different from the pagan world of antiquity and from the world nourished by Christianity. It was a world in which no *mystique* could survive, where Socialism and Catholicism alike were Parties. The de-republicanisation of France and the de-christianisation of France are aspects of the same movement, its 'de-mystification'. But even this modern world, specifically this modern world, which was further than ever before from Christianity, is not permanent, and its indigence is only temporary.

Let this be clearly understood. I do not say for ever . . .
But there we are.
We even have very deep reasons for hoping it will not
be for long.'

In the interval between his first attack on the modern
world and *Notre Jeunesse* he had returned to Catholicism
and in the first version of *Clio* his views are qualified. His
polemic is no less violent, but it is refined and coloured by
the positive aim. All that he had formerly said about the
modern world remains unchanged but his recognition of
the fruits of the Revolution—which he usually failed to
mention—is now expressed in the most challenging form
in order that 'the Christian operation' of nourishing the
world mystically, the Christian mission, should be seen in
the fullest light and set in the realities of the present.

For the first time, for the very first time since Jesus, we have
seen, under our very eyes, we have just seen a new world arise, if
not a city; modern society, the modern world; we have seen a
world, a society constitute itself, or at least assemble, (be born)
and grow, after Jesus, without Jesus. And what is more, my friend
[Clio] adds, more striking, and what must not be denied, is that
they have succeeded.
    That is what confers upon our generation, my child, on your
generation and upon the times in which we live, a supreme importance; that is what places you at a unique point in history. That
is what puts you in a tragic and unique situation. You are the first
. . . the first who have succeeded in making a world, and a prosperous world, without Jesus, a whole society, a prosperous society
without Jesus.

It is as though Péguy's view of the modern world, his
criticism of its delinquencies as well as his recognition of

its achievements only attained their balance and stability when he saw it as a Catholic, as the field in which 'the Christian operation' was to take place. And simultaneously his attack on the Catholics who had witnessed, allowed and condoned the de-christianisation of France became completely open. Their error, their fault rather, is that they would not recognise what is new, the existence of a modern world (I do not say a modern *city*, he adds), and the fact that it lies wholly and entirely outside Christianity. 'The Catholic diagnosis is always a cowardly one which blames and rejects the modern world, which refuses to see what is new and what is true. Even *nos misères*, are no longer Christian.'

That the world should have become Christian presents no problem—faith is never the problem to Péguy and the real difficulty is always hope. The problem is to understand the de-christianisation of the world. And here Péguy reverses the usual procedure of the apologists who blame the de-christianisation of Europe on the evil of the times; he puts the whole blame on the Catholics, and in particular on the clergy, who allowed the idea of tradition to harden so that what should have been the source of new forms of life became an obstacle to change. The existence of 'an eternal foundation, eternal in origin, does not alter the fact that . . . one always has to begin again temporarily speaking.'* In history, *the Church is always at the beginning*. The belief in a static tradition is a failure to understand *creation* itself, and the *clercs* think and act as though history were entirely distinct from creation, as though the Kingdom of God were to follow at once, and not the City of God.

---

*The quotations are from the first *Clio*, p. 235 ff.

That is what they forget too often, what our Clerks generally lose sight of . . . There is a lot of impiety in their ignorance of the times, of the (temporal) centuries; in that more or less voluntary ignorance, more or less involuntary; more or less conscious, but generally quite conscious; in that more or less affected contempt; a lot of pride, certainly, and a lot of laziness; which are both capital sins; but what is much more serious, in a sense infinitely more serious, a great lack of piety . . . an infinite misunderstanding as to what creation is, of what makes creation, of its taste, its real taste on the tongue.

The pages that follow are a furious attack on *La Trahison des clercs* in the opposite sense to that of his friend Julien Benda from whom perhaps he took a hint. It is an attack on the *clercs* for ignoring the movement of history and the signs of the times; for not playing their part; for withdrawing from the world and treating and teaching religion as a withdrawal from the wicked world; or when they take a hand, for doing everything to prevent mysticism from nourishing the City.

One would almost say that their one intention is to wreck the eternal gardens. That their only care in time is, when they see a sign of it, to prevent anything flowering, the flowering of sanctity, the fecundity of the fruits of holiness . . . Their brutality, their tactlessness is frightening, even, and especially where grace is concerned . . . the feet of elephants in the gardens of the Lord.

The only explanation of such a disaster, a mystical disaster, is that there must have been a *mystical* fault.

Their responsibility is huge in having turned their backs on the times, hiding behind the affectation of decrying the times, clinging to the past and afraid of the future, of everything new. The Christian *mystique,* which was meant

to inspire and nourish the world in all its phases, had with-
drawn into private life. *On est épouvanté des responsabilités
qu'ils auront.* For by increasing their authority politically
during the nineteenth century, they had increased their
responsibility.

More precisely, Péguy defines the fault as a 'technical
mystical fault', *une machine en arrière*, as 'mysticism in reverse', moving out of the world and away from the world
instead of into it, to save it.

We only have to read the text of the event . . . The fault of
technique, of mysticism, the inversion, consists quite precisely
[the Muse of history continues] and could only be a *failure to
understand me*, a misunderstanding of me . . . That is the precise
historical fault, the rational fault, the mystical fault . . . The
eternal has (temporarily) aborted in the temporal; [this had been
the source of Joan's despair;] the eternal has been temporarily sus-
pended because those charged with power, those in whom the
power of eternity is founded, have scorned and forgotten and mis-
understood the temporal.

And in his bitterness Péguy concludes that those who
have made so many people say *mea culpa,* whose profession
is to make others say *mea culpa,* will never say it themselves.
They do not want to acknowledge their fault. And as a
result a whole people, which seemed to have become
Christian for ever, has ceased to be Christian. The *clercs*
prefer to sit back and blame everything on the wickedness
of the times, instead of acknowledging that *Tous les temps
sont les temps de Jésus.*

Péguy's sense of tradition and freedom, which provoked
this furious attack on the clergy and the clericals, widened
with his gradual understanding of Catholicity, of the

specifically Catholic expression of Christianity until he
could write that *Tous les temps sont les temps de Jésus.*

The experience recorded in the *Mystery of the Charity of
Joan of Arc* taught him the meaning of Christendom: 'He
is there.' The profoundly irreligious atmosphere of the
modern world is not a matter for pious laments or con-
demnations but the condition in which a living faith must
discover its mission. Nor is it a paradox that the longest
and most intemperate of Péguy's tirades against the
modern world should occur in the poem in which he em-
braces it in his Christian view of history.

In this poem (he says of *Eve*), the tone of infinite respect to
which Péguy has accustomed us will be found once again. That
respect extends not only to the Christian world, it extends to the
world of antiquity and to the modern world. It extends in truth to
the whole universe.

This respect is the burden of the *climate* of heritage which
occupies a central position in the epic.

> *Il allait hériter du monde occidental,*
> *De celui qui se lève aux colonnes d'Hercule,*
> *Il allait hériter d'un foudre ridicule,*
> *Et des débarquements du monde oriental.*

Immediately after the Nativity come the quatrains on
the Lord's heritage, till the whole of history is embraced in
the redemption, and the eternal salvation of man is seen as
the centre of his temporal salvation.

And further (he says in the *Commentary*) it is very difficult not to
consider the world of antiquity, the city of antiquity, Greece and

Rome, as having received a sort of temporal vocation and destiny, as having been charged to prepare that enormous apparatus, the orb of the world under the government of Rome, for Jesus who was about to be born. It is the thesis of Bossuet himself in the *Discours sur l'histoire universelle.*

XII

CLIO AND VERONICA

The intellectual *venue* of Péguy's last duel with the modern world, in the course of which he finally recognised his own situation, is contained in a series of *Cahiers* all having the same title: *De la situation faite à l'histoire* and slightly different sub-titles.*

The theme had first emerged in the early *Cahiers* where Péguy began to investigate the metaphysics of Jaurès and the Socialists and to trace their affinity with Renan and Taine,† the pontiffs of the 'intellectuals'. For it was not Socialism which he was criticising, but the modern world.

People too often forget that the modern world, under another name, is the bourgeois capitalist world. And it is an amusing spectacle to see how our Socialist, our anti-Christian and particularly anti-Catholic Socialists, indifferent to the contradiction, offer incense to the world under the name of modern, and lash it under the name of bourgeois and capitalist.

The world of Jaurès and Guesdes was not fundamentally different from the world of Renan and Taine and their off-

---

De la situation faite à l'histoire et à la sociologie dans les temps modernes (Nov. 1906); *De la situation faite—au parti intellectuel dans le monde moderne* (Dec. 1906), a sequel dated Feb. 1907, and *De la situation faite— au parti intellectuel dans le monde moderne devant les accidents de la gloire temporelle* (Oct. 1907).

†Maurras calls Taine 'our master'. In this context at least, Péguy was justified in regarding the two ideologies of the modern world, the Right and the Left, as at bottom identical.

spring Maurras. The metaphysics of the Left and the Right were at bottom the same. That is how it happens that Péguy's investigation of their metaphysical assumptions begins in *Zangwill* (1904), a masterly essay on Renan and Taine. The theme was dropped during the next two years, but after *Notre Patrie* and *Les Suppliants Parallèles* he returns to the charge in four *Cahiers* where the modern world, its philosophy and its philosophers, the intellectuals, are submitted to an investigation which threatened to be unending. Not only the reader but Péguy himself was bogged, for he had reached the point where his criticism required that he should reveal the situation in which, as a result of the argument, he now found himself. In the silence that followed he began *Clio* and several of the unpublished *Cahiers* dealing with history.

The details, the niceties, the *longueurs* of Péguy's argument lie outside the scope of these notes, and I need only summarise his situation in the baldest terms. The philosophy of the modern world (whether Marxist or Maurassien) is a philosophy of history. They may deny that they have a metaphysic, 'but nothing is so common as metaphysics. *Tout le monde en fait.* Only people have the metaphysics—and the religion—they deserve. Because one has the metaphysics—and the religion (Péguy was at the end of his tether)—of what one is, or, to speak more exactly, which one is.'

The metaphysics of the modern world consists in the thesis that 'we can know, attain, seize and grasp the whole of reality' by means of a technique of notes, of *fiches* correctly disposed and that it provides us with 'an integral knowledge, with an exhaustive grasp' which is both real and metaphysical. In other words history provides all our knowledge and explains everything. That was Renan's claim, who held that, if not yet quite complete, our know-ledge was so far advanced that one could see the end: *mais on voit le bout*. Taine, Péguy had said, made the same claims which he describes in *Zangwill* as 'une usurpation théo-logique':

Renan, more aware, more philosophical, more of an artist, more of a man of the world—and consequently more respectful of the divinity—more hellenic, and consequently more aware that the Gods are jealous of their attributes, Renan, better informed, had only usurped the attributes of an omniscient God; Taine, more self-sufficient, more obstinate, more scholarly, more deeply in-volved, more of a child too, being more of a professor, and above all more complete, usurps the rôle of creation itself; he takes on the work of God the creator.

Taine, with his honesty, let the cat out of the bag. As Acton says:

His fundamental dogma was the denial of free will and the absolute dominion of physical causes over the life of mankind. A violent effort to shape the future by intention and design, and not by causes that are in the past, seemed to him the height of folly. The idea of starting fresh, from the morrow of creation, of eman-cipating the individual from the mass, the living from the dead, was a defiance of the laws of nature.

But each time that Taine or Renan published a book, Péguy comments, it was an acknowledgement that they had renounced the totality of knowledge; like Herodotus, like Plutarch, like Plato they had chosen:

'Chosen, that is the great word; to choose is the method of art.'

History could be an art, but it could not be a science.

Scientific history might claim to be the resurrection of the past, but it became 'the burial of the present in the past'. And, moreover, unless it functioned as an art it could never penetrate the event, for it is not like memory which strikes down into the event. 'Nothing is so contrary to memory as history . . . History is essentially longitudinal; memory is essentially vertical. History *passes along* the event', while memory consists in remaining within it. There are in fact (as Bergson was saying in *Matière et Mémoire*) two memories, the one which notes, which makes its *fiches*, and the memory which re-lives. History, on the contrary, unless it is an art, and creative, only 'considers life at the moment it becomes dead'. It only deals with facts, with *le fait* (that which is made, finished and done with) whereas it is *le se faisant* (what is in the making) which reveals the nature of reality and the mystery of the present.

These *Cahiers* break off in the autumn of 1907. But Péguy, though he published nothing, took up the theme again in his return to Catholicism intending to write two *Cahiers* in which to sum up all he had said about History and all that he now could add.

The first volume will be called *Clio*. The second will be called *Veronica* . . . Clio spends her time looking for the imprints of the past, vain imprints; and a little Jewess, a little nobody, a child, Veronica, takes out her handkerchief and takes an eternal imprint of the face of Jesus. *Voilà ce qui enfonce tout.*

It was not history that explained Christianity, but Christianity which explained history. But in the interval, Péguy had got on excellent terms with Clio, and she talked to him with all the frankness and honesty of Taine, and the irony and grace of Renan:

J'ai fait, dit-elle, (comme) soucieuse, et se parlant à elle-même tout en commençant de m'adresser la parole; ruminant en soi-même; mâchant des paroles de ses vieilles dents historiques, marmottante; marmonnante; mâchonnante; soucieuse, ayant pris soudain un air sérieux, comme pour de rire, les sourcils froncés, le front froncé, j'ai fait de travail moi-même. On n'est jamais si bien servi que par moi-même.

Véronique was never even begun, partly no doubt because Péguy had struck such a happy vein in *Clio* that he wrote it in two entirely different forms. But in its place there is *Eve*, his *discours sur l'histoire universelle*, in which the poet expresses the metaphysic—and the religion—which he opposes to the determinist metaphysics of the modern world. And it is not Veronica who speaks but the Incarnation himself:

> *Jésus parle.*
> *O Mère ensevelie hors du premier jardin,*
> *Vous n'avez plus connu ce climat de la grâce*
> *Et la vasque et la source et la haute terrasse*
> *Et le premier soleil sur le premier matin.*
>
> *Et les bondissements de la biche et du daim*
> *Nouant et dénouant leur course fraternelle*
> *Et courant et sautant et s'arrêtant soudain*
> *Pour mieux commémorer leur vigueur éternelle*
>
> *Ce qui depuis ce jour est devenu la somme*
> *S'obtenait sans total et sans addition*
> *Et la sagesse assise au coteau de Sion*
> *N'eût point depareillé l'ange d'avecque l'homme.*
>
> *Et Dieu lui-même jeune ensemble qu'éternel*
> *Regardait ce que c'est que le temps de l'année.*
> *Immuable il voyait d'un regard paternel*
> *Passer parmi ses soeurs la saison couronnée.*

It was not History, but Revelation which should speak of the Alpha and the Omega, and in *Eve* history is illuminated by revelation and reflecting the light which it receives deepens his understanding of history.

XIII

LAST WORDS

At the end of his life Péguy was 'under observation', for it was felt that, with his love of freedom, he might at any moment make a mistake, and his enemies preferred a safe half-truth to the whole truth with its inevitable dangers. In the *Note Conjointe*, the last of the *Cahiers*, Péguy wrote his testament. 'By word of mouth,' he had said to Fernand Laudet in *Un Nouveau Théologien*: 'By word of mouth I am still capable of lying like everyone else . . . But the moment I have a pen in hand, I don't say I do not wish to lie; I say I cannot lie any more.' And in the dialogue that concludes the *Note Conjointe*, he said all he had to say to his friends, Catholics and Protestants, Jews and Free-thinkers, to all those who acknowledged the truth of his faith and his love of freedom. For the last time, and not without irony, he explains how freedom and Catholicism are one, and that his belief in the unity of Catholicism was the fruit of his belief in freedom.

The end of the *Note Conjointe* is in the form of a dialogue between Péguy and an interlocutor who suddenly appears from nowhere, a Monsignor as it turns out, who comes to ask one or two little questions. For Péguy was aware that the Catholic attack on Bergson exposed him to their suspicion. Earlier in the book, he had already said what he had to say about the attitude of certain Catholics to Bergson: it was 'an essentially political attitude' and, moreover, he adds, the attack is tactically futile:

Everything that is lost by Bergson [as a result of his condemnation, that is] will not be gained by Saint Thomas, but regained by Spencer.

Agreed—people reply, but it was necessary to put Bergson on the index. It was the only way of preventing his being read in the Seminaries. He was turning the heads of all the young men there. [And at this point the *Cahier* breaks into a dialogue.]

And then you know quite well what the index is . . . it's only . . . well it's just a list, a list which, after all, one is compelled . . . And, moreover, one can get as many dispensations as one likes. The index is simply an indication.

— I'm sorry, you have got it wrong: in point of fact I do not know what the index is exactly. And I should like to add that I have no desire to enter, incidentally, into the great debate between Bergson and the Catholics . . .

First of all I must admit that it is true that I do not know exactly what the index is. And even, in a sense, that I don't know at all. The reason after all is perfectly simple. At bottom I only know what was in the catechism when I was a child. In my catechism there was God, the creation, sacred history; the blessed Virgin, the angels and the saints; the calendar, the great feasts; prayer and the sacraments; the virtues, the symbol of the apostles; the last end of man (which in those days seemed a long way off) . . . and the seven deadly sins. There was no index . . . And even today I still cannot conceive it at all, because it was not there.

— But if we talked about it, today, perhaps you could form some conception of it.

And Péguy's dialogue is launched.

— I'm not very quick.
— But all the same if it were explained to you . . .
— It would be kinder to talk of other things.
— You would perhaps be able to imagine it.
— One can imagine things up to twelve, you know. After twelve

one can no longer imagine anything. After twelve one is no longer
a poet. All that I failed to imagine the morning of my first com-
munion I shall never be able to imagine.
— One might perhaps try to explain that . . .
— Be careful. I am old. And hard-headed. A *Beauceron.*
— Perhaps one might be able to . . .

And in spite of ten more pages of the same treatment
the Monsignor never loses patience. He is very sure of
turning the corner.

— Well, the Index is only an indication. Like the signposts by the
road-side.
— That (Péguy admits) is my weak spot. You have found my
weak spot. There is nothing so beautiful as the open road, well
signed and posted: *Chartres* 41 *kilomètres* . . . Of course they are
necessary. But are they useful?
— What, my child, are the indications not indispensable?
— In the realm of utility, *Monseigneur.* One can see you have
never been along the road. Now I guarantee, being in Paris,
I guarantee to go to Chartres without consulting the signposts,
and without looking at the milestones.
— *Parbleu,* then you know the road.
— One always knows it. What I mean is: there is always someone
who knows it for you . . . Believe me, Father (and here his voice
took on a certain distance, and gravity and melancholy), I have
walked the road, I've been on the road to Chartres. Allow me to
tell you that what makes one go to Chartres are not the milestones or the signposts.
— Then what, my child?
— The wooden crosses at the corner of the road . . . And one
doesn't need an inscription to tell one where one is.
    The priest felt the shot; and showed that it had gone home. He
was silent for a long time, as though he, too, were pursuing grave
and melancholy thoughts. Already far away. Then he smiled, for

he loved that son of his, strong, half-rebel, wholly docile, whose
fidelity could not be computed, and whose solidity was proof
against every trial.

— Well, he said, well, and what about consulting the road-signs
at the cross-roads?

— We've got there at last, *Monseigneur*, we're coming to the
point, the conclusion, our destination. At last we're going to see
what a Catholic is.

He looked at me surprised.

— But this demands, I continued, a certain . . . a certain delicacy.

He made a sign to say that he did not doubt it.

— All the more so, I continued, since we are entering an altogether
strange realm.

— . . .

— No, no, it is not the realm of Catholicity that is foreign. We are
entering, I continued imperturbably, an unknown domain, a
strange realm, the domain of joy. A hundred times less known, a
hundred times more strange, than the kingdom of sorrow. A hundred times more profound, I believe, and a hundred times more
fertile. How happy the ones who some day have some conception
of it. It's a joy to march along the road, a very mysterious and profound phenomenon to read the signposts. One knows perfectly
well where one is going, and what one is passing. One knows quite
well where one is, *ubi, quo, unde, qua*. All the same one goes up to
the signpost by the road-side and looks at it. It does one good, it's
one of the joys of the road. Can you explain that?

Well, a Catholic is a man who knows quite well he is on the
right spiritual road, and who all the same feels the need to consult
the signposts.

Or rather experiences a deep joy in doing so.

When one's principal friends, *Monseigneur*, have been Protestants and Jews, as has been the case with me, one soon begins to
see that they cannot conceive what a Catholic is. And the Protestants are even farther away, more incapable of conceiving what
it is like, than the Jews. They believe they understand him, that

they are opposed to him, fight against him. In reality, however, they not only don't know him, they do not understand him and cannot see him. The particular sort of gratuity which there is in the Catholic. And here we are touching on one of the discriminating points, one of the points that mark the difference, one of the points at which Protestants cannot conceive what a Catholic is. Protestants are people who make their own signposts. And they not only make them, they justify them all the time.

The Catholic, on the contrary (do I make myself quite clear: only Catholics will understand me), the Catholic is a man who arrives on the road and finds that the signposts put there for everyone suit him very well. And more than that, the signposts are there for everyone—he does not have to consult them to know the way. He knows the road well enough, he knows it, he sees it, and does like everyone else. The road is clear enough to see. He consults the signposts in order to feel a certain joy, one of the ritual joys of the road, to accomplish a certain rite, the rite of the road.

. . . A particular ritual joy that cannot be communicated to others.

A useless, gratuitous, superfluous joy.

The only joy.

All the rest are paid for.

That is the one profound (the only irrevocable) failure of communication between the Catholic and the rest (the Jew a little less, all the same). The Catholic follows the rest. And in the meanwhile each Protestant sets up his own signposts . . .

The Catholic consults the signposts for the sake of consulting them. The Protestant

Saturday, August 1st, 1914.

Péguy was interrupted in the middle of a sentence by the news of the mobilisation. He was cut short in his work, but he had lived long enough to have experienced the mysterious joy of being on the right road, the joy which freedom brought him as it merged into the unity he had pursued all his life, the joy of their harmony. 'Happy the man who one day has some conception of it.'

Heureux ceux qui sont morts pour la terre charnelle
Pourvu que ce soit dans une juste guerre.

XIV

EPILOGUE

C'est une renaissance catholique qui se fait par moi.

During his lifetime and in the years immediately follow-ing on his death, Péguy's work met with an extremely varied reception. The most general, and the most honest, was one of bewilderment, which was easily translated into regarding him as an eccentric. Politics and religion, socialism and nationalism, not to mention freedom and tradition, jostled one another in his pages. Nor did his Catholicism supply the necessary label. Péguy himself had not made the task of understanding his work easy. He kept his secret to himself, and never showed more than one side of his many-sided mind to his friends.

It was not until twenty-five years after his death that fashion caught up with him. A few lines of his poetry, some of the high-lights of the *Cahiers,* and a sentimental picture of the old Socialist who made a pilgrimage to Chartres and died on the battlefield sufficed to provide the cult with an object. But the fashion was also a sign that times had changed, and in the new atmosphere Péguy's work was no longer seen as disjointed and eccentric. What now emerged as the most striking quality was the unity and consistency of his thought, and its central position.

It does not seem as though Péguy's work contributed to any serious extent in bringing about the change. He was better understood, because his readers were better pre-pared to grasp his meaning. *Tu ne me lirais pas si tu ne m'avais déjà compris* still applies, with special force, to Péguy, and it is only since about 1940 that the work of sifting his ideas has begun.

This could only happen when interest in his work had reached the point where it corresponded to Péguy's conception of his rôle: *C'est une renaissance catholique qui se fait par moi:* when the Catholics began to recognise in Péguy's work an echo of their own hopes. As Bernanos was careful to say, Péguy is 'a man who answers when one speaks to him'. But Péguy's words to Lotte may prove as great a snare to his unwary admirers as to his more critical reader. Once the *par moi* is stressed too much, the false quantity alters his meaning. He had in fact made the easy mistake himself, and in the first moment of excitement he thought he had only to hand out his poems to be elected to the Academy and welcomed as a leader by the true fold. He was quickly undeceived and learnt the lesson Pascal taught Domat when he wrote that 'our mission is not to make the truth triumph, but to fight for it'.

When Péguy referred to a Catholic renaissance he was not talking in the air. He only had to look about him to see that after a period of sterility, Catholicism in France was beginning to stir. All the fields which had lain fallow showed signs of life, even though the forms it took were not always to his liking. Theology, philosophy, history and letters were in a state of ferment, enlivened by the work of Laberthonière, Blondel, Maritain, Duchesne, Bremond, Psichari and Claudel. Bloy he would not have included. But whatever Péguy's criticism, particularly where Modernism was concerned, the renaissance he had in mind was not a figment of his imagination. It was a reality; and although he did not trouble himself overmuch about its achievements, he believed it had a future.

Indeed his faith in the future made him suspicious of immediate results. He was in no hurry; he was not impatient and he does not sound the apocalyptic note which he found so irritating in Bloy. A renaissance could not be arranged from today or tomorrow. *Ne mettez point la main sur le fruit qui n'est pas mur.* Ripeness was not everything if it held no promise for the future. But in time the renaissance Péguy saw 'in thought at least' during his last years, caught up with him, and recognised his true value.

Shortly after the publication of *The Holy Innocents* Lotte evidently thought that the situation was ripe for action. He wrote to Péguy and suggested he should put himself at the head of a 'traditionalist' movement: a good example of how not to understand the *par moi* :

You can readily imagine, Péguy replied, that you are not the only one, and I can in fact see a whole movement, in thought at least, at the head of which I could put myself. That is precisely what I do not want. I have the gravest personal reasons for not agreeing to have greatness of any kind, even spiritual, thrust upon me. I know perfectly well what my office is and what it is not.

Today is the feast of Joan of Arc at Orleans, and I am not there. It will always be so. My task is to furnish a career of suffering and sorrow and to draw from it what you know.

Lotte is surely not to be blamed. Péguy had used and continued to use his *Bulletin* to make himself known, and the terms in which he spoke of his own works are unsurpassed in the annals of self-praise. He had even reason to think that Lotte needed to be warned not to confuse Péguy's admiration for his own poetry and his office:

It is extremely important, he wrote again, not to dub me a Father of the Church. It is quite enough to be one of her sons.

That is the folly which has happened in Brunetière's case. It means banquets and speeches. There is absolutely nothing in common between Brunetière's history and mine.

It was now extremely important not to talk of him as a *maître*, not to identify him with a party or his work with a 'movement'. The unity of the *Mysteries*, he explained, consisted in the fact that they expressed *la chrétienté dans la paroisse*, the Christianity of the parish, of the community. This was no new development. As early as 1899, when he found himself at loggerheads with the Socialists he wrote that his friends would not desert him 'because,' he said, 'I should only be their manifestation.' And now, in the same way, he regarded his office as being to manifest the nature of a renaissance. *Par moi* has no other meaning. His mission required that he should express the norm as fully as possible. And in the last pages which he wrote he described all that this involved: he was not a Father of the Church, but a son, 'half rebel, wholly docile, whose fidelity could not be computed'. There was nothing he 'loved so much as liberty' except its form, order, discipline and the rule.

It is true, he writes to Dom Baillet, that I should regard it as a great joy to be able to talk to you in peace; but as long as I am not dying, I should have great scruples in withdrawing you, if only for a short time, from the rule of your Order. I have such a feeling and such admiration for the Rule; living in the world, I submit myself to such strict rules of morality, work, prayer, suffering and poverty, I have such an admiration for your Rule, and so much like your being there, that I should scruple to break it, even though it were for my own sake.

I leave on the 28th to do my military service.

To have allowed himself to head a movement, or to become involved in forming a party, could only have narrowed and limited the 'renaissance' and have accentuated the *par moi*. Moreover, the formation of a party could only have suggested that the freedom, which was its condition and its life, was in some sense the antithesis of obedience, instead of representing 'Christendom in the parish'. Freedom and obedience belonged together, and to separate them was to fall back either into the sterility of order, as he says in the *Commentary*, or the fecundity of disorder. Péguy's task was to guarantee the integrity of his work by furnishing a career of suffering in order to 'draw from it what you know'. He might have followed Kierkegaard when, speaking of his mission, he wrote: *Credidi propter quod locutus sum; ego autem humiliatus sum nimis.* Péguy believed and therefore he had spoken, but he himself was humbled by suffering.

Péguy confided his understanding of his 'office' to Lotte, but he did not, it seems certain, initiate him into the secret of his suffering.

> *Laurent, serrez ma haire*
> *Soyez discret.*
> *Il faut qu'un pauvre hère*
> *Reste secret.*

With a grim irony Péguy uses the well-known lines in which Tartuffe makes his hosts believe that he wears a hair shirt, in order to conceal his own. He is the wretched man who must conceal his private suffering in order to 'draw from it what you know', putting his life at the disposal of his office. Since the appearance of the *Quatrains* and the *Sonnets* the suffering they refer to has been made known. At a time when his family life was still racked by the disagreements following on his conversion, Péguy had fallen in love with a young girl who frequented the circle that gathered round him at the *Cahiers*. And Péguy, secure in his righteousness, confident in his faithfulness to the moral law, was suddenly bowled over by a whirlwind of passion.

> *Tu avais tout pourvu*
> *Fors cette fièvre*
> *Tu avais tout prévu*
> *Fors ces deux lèvres*
>
> *Tu avais tout pourvu*
> *Fors cette flamme*
> *Tu avais tout prévu*
> *Fors une autre âme.*
>
> *O cœur plein d'un seul amour*
> *Dissuadé*
> *O cœur de jour en jour*
> *Plus obsédé.*

It was in the summer of 1910. *Ce fut, dans sa vie, un terrible ouragan,* Madame Geneviève Favre (Maritain's mother) wrote—one of the two people in whom he confided his torment. The storm lasted through the summer, till in September he could write to Madame Favre 'Je travaille à bloc pour me mettre à la raison. J'en ai été un peu malade, mais j'aime mieux être un peu malade de travail que de manquer ma vocation par un dérèglement du cœur.' He had had the courage to persuade the girl he loved to marry. Perhaps she never knew the violence of the feelings she had aroused.

Péguy's decision was, like all his decisions, total and

final; and the completeness of his sacrifice gave him back his freedom; *le bonheur* was less than *l'honneur*.

> *Le jeune enfant bonheur*
> *Vint en courant.*
> *Mais le seigneur honneur*
> *Parut plus grand.*

It was then that Péguy wrote to Lotte, 'Everything is as it should be: incredible suffering in the private sphere; immense graces for my production.'

Péguy's poetry cannot be interpreted in terms of his life; it is his poetry which provides the framework in which his life, and in particular the great moral crisis through which he went, can be seen in the right perspective. He says, on one occasion, and there is no reason to doubt his honesty, that he only understood the *Mystery of the Holy Innocents* after he had written it: *The Innocents,* he wrote to Lotte, 'was an anticipation. I had never practised what I expressed there. Now I abandon myself.' He was thinking no doubt of the passage in the invocation to night:

> He who abandons himself does not abandon himself, and
>   he is the only one who does not abandon himself . . .
> Now you, my daughter night . . .
> You are the only one who can sometimes conquer that
>   rebel and bend his stubborn neck.

It was not through any desire to demonstrate his consistency and so justify his past, that Péguy refused to allow that he had been converted. The nature of the renaissance he believed it was his office to manifest, is in fact distorted unless his premise is granted. He did not return to Catholicism and subsequently elaborate a theory, a renaissance.

What Péguy discovered in the course of his *approfondisse-ment* was the condition of a renaissance, and he had no need to deny his past, the path on which he had been, when he found that it was the Christian path. This becomes evident the moment his work is seen in retrospect and as a whole instead of broken up into successive phases.

Péguy began as a militant Socialist. But in the first *Cahier,* when his disagreement with the Socialists forced him to begin examining what he meant by freedom, he made the distinctive colour of his Socialism clear. 'The revolution will be moral or it will not happen.' To men like Herr and Blum this meant only one thing. Péguy was turning his back on Socialism and retreating into the last ditch of bourgeois individualism: freedom and morality in that form meant anarchy; it was a diseased bourgeois love of freedom. Yet at first sight a 'moral revolution' still appeared to be a revolution within Socialism, and Péguy was what would now be called a deviationist, recalling Socialism to its origins, and maintaining the rights and value of the individual in face of the devouring, abstract collectivism of Marxist doctrine.

But as it wound its way through the *Cahiers* the revolution he was fighting for drew Péguy deeper and deeper into its grasp. He had assumed that morality and ethics were beyond discussion till he began to discuss them. It was then that he discovered that his moral revolution was in fact a revolution in the morals, in the generally accepted moral ideas of his contemporaries.

What was at stake was the reality of freedom: which he saw denied in theory by the determinist philosophy of Socialism, and in practice by the Catholic Party with its antagonism to the modern world. He found himself in opposition to Socialist metaphysics (the metaphysics of

Jaurès) and to Catholic practice. But he maintained that if they were true to their *mystique* they would not have found themselves in irreconcilable opposition, and that their *politiques* would have been modified.

Péguy's moral revolution was a return to the traditional moral values of Catholicism; it began as a criticism of the Socialist Party, and ended as a criticism of the Catholic Party. In essence a criticism of the fundamental weakness of nineteenth-century Catholicism in France. The reality of freedom, Péguy maintained, was poised on the traditional equilibrium between nature and grace and the health and vitality of the 'Christian operation' depended on the right relation between grace and free-will, the one true freedom.

During the nineteenth century the ethos of Catholicism had been subtly altered, and permeated by individualism, which is the soil in which Jansenism flourishes. The pessimistic political view of the Catholic bourgeoisie, the mathematical certainty of their decreasing political power, had encouraged a pessimistic view of human nature. And since their opponents, the Liberals and Progressives, proclaimed the natural goodness of man, they slipped into the habit of stressing the weakness of man and their Christianity made more of his *misère* than of his *grandeur*. Their pessimism was not, like that of the Jansenists, a protest against a lax and worldly religion, but a defence of their refusal to participate in the life of the country—a *ressentiment*. Unwilling and perhaps unable to establish any fruitful links with the contemporary world, they confined morality to the private sphere. Their tactics, Péguy says, consisted in 'fraudulently abasing' nature in the belief that by reducing the stature of man they were magnifying the stature of God. 'Because they have no temporal courage they think they have penetrated into the eternal. Because they love no one, they think they love God.'*

Freedom in that atmosphere was suspect; not of course 'the freedom of the will' operating within the private sphere, but the practical creative freedom which to Péguy is the life-blood of tradition. Instead of informing tradition and giving it form (*du nouveau réelle*), it was mistrusted as in danger of kicking over the traces; and thus obedience, separated from freedom, came to mean obedience to the existing and outworn forms of tradition. That was the attitude of mind which Péguy described as 'mysticism in reverse'.

The strangeness of Péguy's work is no doubt due to some extent to the revolution in morals out of which it sprang. The absence of the Jansenistic stop, which in many modern Catholic writers is the theological device, so to

---

*Since Péguy wrote, his criticisms have often been taken up, and are no longer a novelty. One example must suffice to show that Péguy is by no means eccentric at this point.

'There developed,' Dr. Pieper writes, 'especially in the "Christian middle classes", an unsound over-valuation of moderation (temperance), to the point at which modern usage has confined the notion of morality almost exclusively to this partial sphere. As a result of the middle class exteriorisation of this virtue (temperance), the word morality has acquired an ironic and derogatory connotation . . . The confinement of the ethical to the private sphere, quite obviously originates in individualism. The classical theology of the Church ranks temperance as the last and lowest of the cardinal virtues, for the explicit reason that it relates solely to the individual.'

The essay from which this quotation is taken, 'Fortitude and Temperance' (Faber), provides an interesting commentary on Péguy's moral revolution. Dr. Pieper shows the extent to which individualism, while encouraging an optimistic view of human nature outside the Church, produced the contrary effect within it. The forms which the perversion of the traditional doctrine took are compared with the teaching of Aquinas and the Fathers, and the comparison reveals the fullness of Péguy's return to tradition.

say, by which the supernatural is introduced, alters the whole tonality of his work, giving it the full range which he needed in order to express his respect, to recall his phrase, for nature and grace. If the 'hurricane' which threatened Péguy's moral life was introduced at this point and not earlier, it was to emphasise that Péguy's work was not written from an ivory tower, or by a man who did not know the meaning of passion. But it was not the tension between nature and grace which provided the tension in his work. He did not make use of the sacrifice which he made as a door-way to the eternal. The choice between *le bonheur* and *l'honneur* was first of all a choice on the natural plane.

One of Péguy's bewildering idiosyncrasies is his opinion of Corneille. Even his French critics find his admiration for Corneille, whom he puts above every other poet except possibly Sophocles, excessive. But Péguy did not hesitate. 'I shall never equal Polyeuct,' he writes as though even he could hardly hope to recover and express the dignity of man, and as though Corneille were the last poet to write before the incoming tide of Jansenism and individualism had swamped and eaten into the roots of man's freedom.

Polyeuct, he says, admires Sévère like a man who knows what he is talking about; his Christian greatness is founded on surpassing, not on ignoring, pagan greatness. His sanctity is founded on surpassing, not on ignoring, the heroism of antiquity. His God is founded on surpassing, not on ignoring, or looking with a certain contempt upon, the world.

Corneille is Péguy's ideal because he expressed the traditional equilibrium between human nature and grace on which a genuine freedom ultimately rests.

Liberty must go to meet grace. Man is a besieged city. Sin is that perfectly ordered blockade. Grace is that royal army marching to the rescue. But the liberty of man must make a sortie, *erumpat*, and go to meet the relieving army.

Péguy's conversion was a sortie; his freedom went, as it were, to meet the grace which had stolen upon him 'insidiously', which came unexpectedly because it never takes the same path twice, being 'the source of all freedom'. But that movement, the fulfilment of his 'moral revolution', became, in the light of grace, the condition of renaissance. He could only say that he denied nothing of his past, least of all his Socialism. For while he wanted to inoculate Socialism with a true individualism, he equally wanted to purge Catholicism of its false individualism.

Péguy, in fact, was not afraid of Socialism, but for it. He was afraid that the narrow metaphysics to which it was tied (like Jaurès) would suffocate its *mystique,* its faith in liberty, and that it would become a sterile ideology, a plan or various modifications of a plan, exploited by demagogues. For unless man is really free, he cannot be given freedom, and everything he creates imprisons him. The moral revolution which he said was the *sine qua non* of Socialism, was a return to its *mystique,* the faith which created Socialism, faith in the genuine freedom of man.

The 'renaissance' which is manifested in his poetry is not a plan for the future, but hope in the future. And from the moment Péguy grasped his 'office' he was like a man possessed. There was only one thing to do: *il faut créer, il faut produir*.

The poetry which he poured out during the next, the last six years, is strangely remote from private interests, and with the exception of the *Sonnets* and the *Quatrains* it is not the suffering of his private life which is its main-spring. 'We are entering an altogether strange realm,' he says in the last pages he was to write, 'we are entering an unknown domain, the domain of joy. A hundred times more strange than the kingdom of sorrow. A hundred times more profound, I believe, and a hundred times more fertile.'

What Péguy creates in the *Mysteries* and in *Eve* is the climate of Christianity, a living language in which the unity of the spiritual life and the spiritual proposition is echoed in the unity of idea and image. Since the seventeenth century (and here Péguy includes even Pascal), men had reasoned, demonstrated and explained too much. Christianity had lost touch with a powerful faculty in man, the imagination, and it tended to become 'rationalism for the few and magic for the many'.* An excess of reasoning had narrowed and confined reason to what could be expressed in a univocal, discursive, mathematical language. Christianity had not only become the religion of the few, of the well-to-do, but of 'intellectuals' whose literature and culture, more and more restricted in its appeal, had ceased to be popular. That culture could not be 'popularised', and no attempt to simplify it could make it popular as long as there was no language to bridge the gulf between the few and the many.

When Romain Rolland read the *Mysteries* on their first appearance, he could find no other way of describing their originality than by saying (in his *Journal*) that after reading Péguy even the greatest contemporary writers sounded 'literary'. The same thing has been said many times since, too often with the intention of praising Péguy at the expense of others, and of comparing his poetry with the

*Burckhardt, *Reflections on History*.

'literary' poetry of the period. Rolland's feeling in fact conveys an important truth, but only so long as his words are taken as an attempt to define the character of Péguy's poetry, and not to grade him. What he says is only one way, and not perhaps the best, of stressing the fact that while his poetry is remote from private interests, Péguy's poetry and his office are fused into a single whole. The poet and his office can of course be investigated in isolation, but his poetry, in the last analysis, is the expression of his office. To study them apart is essential, but to keep them apart is a sure way of not reaching a complete understanding of his work.

It has already been suggested that Coleridge's notion of the imagination, and in general his conception of poetry, is a profitable starting-point in considering Péguy's work. The absence of 'literary' affiliations, the straightforward, 'un-poetic' diction, the complete break with the tradition of French poetry as it runs through Baudelaire, Rimbaud and Mallarmé (as well as the not inconsiderable debt to Hugo), even suggests a comparison with the aims and achievements of Wordsworth. Moreover, Coleridge's theory of the imagination, as long as it is not cut down to fit contemporary taste, leaves room for an examination of the central problem in Péguy's work.

In his study of Péguy, André Rousseaux attacks the question head on. 'Péguy,' he says, 'may be compared to a prophet because from a certain point of view poetry and prophecy are the same.' In English-speaking countries this sort of claim is not warmly received, and the bare mention of the word prophet creates an insurmountable barrier—perhaps a prejudice—which an introduction ought possibly to circumvent, instead of facing squarely. But however the problem is stated, the fact is there, and a

disingenuous attempt to avoid it is not likely to clarify
Péguy's position.

The word prophet is, if anything, more dangerous to
handle than the word mystic; the images and prejudices
which it raises can never all be seized and silenced at once,
they are as uncontrollable as the Hydra. In the first place
there is no certain method of ensuring that the Old Testament idea of the Prophet, looking towards the future, is
decapitated for good; it is certain to raise its head again.
But there is one practicable foothold from which it may
be possible to tame the word. In the First Epistle to the
Corinthians St. Paul contrasts the gift of tongues and the
gift of prophecy, from which it would almost seem that
what is currently meant (or not meant) by prophecy is
more nearly the gift of tongues. The man who speaks with
tongues, St. Paul says (I quote the Revised Version) speaks
'not unto men but unto God; for no man understandeth
him'.

But he that prophesieth speaketh unto men to edification, and
exhortation, and comfort.

Those who speak with tongues, we are told, edify themselves; 'but he that prophesieth edifieth the Church.' It is
that limited, precise and simple definition of prophecy that
can be helpful in defining the character of Péguy's poetry.

Péguy's remark that Pascal reasoned too much, and that
one must not demonstrate and explain but *create* is elaborated in a long passage in *Notre Jeunesse* on the weakness of
Catholic thought and apologetics. 'It is not arguments that
are lacking,' he concludes, 'but charity.' It is not arguments
which he has to offer, but poetry. And the line of his
thought is that charity, in this perspective, is the source of
his office and his poetry. The link between the two is per-

haps given in the opening verse of the Epistle to the
Corinthians: 'Follow after charity and desire spiritual gifts,
but rather that ye may prophesy.' And if Péguy's poetry
is prophecy (in the sense defined above) it may be con-
ceded that his 'office' and his 'poetry' are fused together
legitimately.

If one looks at the sequence of Péguy's poetry the interpretation given does not seem forced. In the *Mystery of the
Charity of Joan of Arc*, with which his poetic work begins,
Joan's charity is the source of her mission, and her work
'follows after charity'. In Péguy's thought the movement
repeats itself, and the 'office' which is born of charity in
the first *Mystery,* proceeds at once to express itself in the
next two *Mysteries* whose theme is hope, courage and comfort. Péguy's renaissance begins, as has been seen, by edify-
ing: by rebuilding the Christian image of man, and he calls
it a system of courage. In this sense the word prophet,
which is so often applied to him as a form of praise, or as
a way of avoiding the need for critical investigation, can
be used to define his work more closely.

But the problem it raises is not only one of attaching a
precise meaning to 'prophecy' (in itself a Herculean task),
and then loosening and expanding the current conception
of poetry, so that they are no longer mutually exclusive.
The other aspect of the problem requires the re-introduc-
tion of the idea of prophecy into contemporary Christianity, and what is no less exacting, the reintroduction of
poetry. Those are among the issues raised by Péguy's
work.

For more than a century, Catholicism in France
had been quiescent, existing within its bulwarks. Paradoxical as it may seem, the more successfully it preserved its
isolation, and refused to enter into the social and political

and cultural movements of the period, the lower its resistance to infection. When, in Péguy's terms, it lacked charity to the extent of ceasing to be creative, it abandoned the main root of tradition and was cut off from the spiritual gifts upon which a renaissance depends. Its thought forms were static where Péguy's are dynamic.

The significance of Péguy's renaissance is best seen, in the first instance, in its bold use of language to bridge the widening gulf which divided France—not primarily the perpendicular cleavage between Clerical and anti-Clerical, the gulf dividing those whom he lumped together as 'intellectuals', but the wider gulf which revealed the full extent of the de-christianisation of France, or as he would say its 'de-mystification': the impassable gulf between the 'intellectuals' and the many, which neither technical language nor literary language could, by definition, hope to bridge. His poetry in this sense is popular.

From this point of view the renaissance manifested in and through his language was the fulfilment of the Socialism he never denied. 'Our Socialism,' he says, in *Notre Jeunesse*, 'was always profoundly spiritual—little as I like the word.' 'Spiritual' to Péguy implied the wrong type of mysticism, 'mysticism in reverse' divorced from action, incapable of creation. The 'Catholic renaissance' it was his office to manifest, was spiritual in the same sense as his Socialism. The temporal salvation of man and the eternal salvation of man are reconciled in the Catholic renaissance he reveals in his poetry:

> *Le monde est bien. Le monde est bien fait. Très bien fait.*
> *Le monde est beau, le monde est grand, le monde est*
> *   bon, le monde est bien, le monde est jeune, le monde est neuf.*
> *Le monde est nouveau.*
> *La création est toute neuve; toute enfant.*

Que toute humanité se fasse chrétienté.
Que la chrétienté croisse au cœur d' humanité
Que toute chrétienté croisse en humanité
Que cette chrétienté se fasse humanité.

Cette prière insensée; comme si j' en avais le droit.
Comme si ça me regardait.
De quoi je me mêlais.
Comme si les affaires du royaume me regardaient.

Quand je pense que j' ai osé avoir un secret avec vous
Quand je pense que je vous ai forcé à avoir un secret avec moi.
Quand je pense que j' ai fait monter vers vous cette
  prière insensée et que je vous ai forcé à l' entendre.

From the second part of the *Mystery of the Charity of Joan of Arc,* posthumously published in the Pléiade edition of the *Oeuvres Poétiques.*